CW01642106

To all of the hurting kids who go to bed every night feeling unloved, and to all of the hurting parents who have gone through similar problems in their childhood. I hope you can find healing through God.

To Ann Storey, who worked tirelessly for me in so many ways.

To Pastor Phil Nordin, for his obedience to God as he builds a church that reaches out to newcomers, to the hurting, and to those in need.

To the people at Jubilee Church, who made me feel welcome in the house of God and in their homes.

To my loving mother, who never stopped praying for me, even during the most difficult times in my life.

To my beloved wife and children, who stood by me and loved me in my most difficult times before I received my healing.

Especially to my beloved grandmother, who took me into her home and gave me unconditional love, which turned my life around from being an outcast.

To Lisa, Rob, Tina, James, Ted and Susan who have enriched my life and my family's life in immeasureable ways.

Throwaway Children

Library and Archives Canada Cataloguing in Publication

VanRiper, Greg, 1967-

Throwaway children / Greg VanRiper.

ISBN 978-1-55452-368-9

1. VanRiper, Greg, 1967-. 2. Adult child abuse victims--Canada--Biography. 3. Christian biography--Canada. I. Title.

RC569.5.C55V37 2009 616.85'822390092 C2009-901770-9

LSI edition 978-1-4600-0027-4 E-book edition: 978-1-4600-0028-1

For more information, please contact:

Greg Van Riper
66 Canoe Circle
Airdrie, AB T4B 2L6
www.gregvanriper.com

Guardian Books is an imprint of *Essence Publishing*, a Christian Book Publisher dedicated to furthering the work of Christ through the written word. For more information, contact:

20 Hanna Court, Belleville, Ontario, Canada K8P 5J2
Phone: 1-800-238-6376 • Fax: (613) 962-4711
E-mail: info@essence-publishing.com
Web site: www.essence-publishing.com

table of contents

My close friend, Rob Walsh, says this all the time and it is my favorite saying:

"I have a wash board stomach…
but there's a load of laundry on top."

Thank you to Cindy, Sherrill and all of the people who worked behind the scenes to help make this book a success.

preface

I know there are people who have been through what I have and worse. I have seen some of them in the institutions and foster homes I lived in. I have also seen them on the streets and in many other places. Their stories are written on their faces, and sometimes they appear to be very defeated. Hopefully some of these people will be fortunate enough to get help at some point in their lives. Whether they reach out for help or someone offers them assistance, the end result, I pray, will be the same, that they will eventually be at peace with their own lives, with others, and with God.

We all have one thing in common: we all go through crises.

As you read about the struggles I went through I pray that it will give you hope. My story is not one of defeat but of victory and how I overcame very difficult situations:

My parents divorced when I was nine.

I was sent into foster care at age twelve.

I was severely abused mentally and physically for two years.

I suffered from an attachment disorder.

I almost froze to death once when I ran away from a foster home.

I had panic attacks and night terrors for years, into adult life and even after I married.

I had two motor vehicle accidents and broke my neck in one.

We had a fire in our house in between the accidents.

We dealt with four deaths in our family within the period that the accidents occurred.

I have been through bankruptcy.

I was separated from my wife for a time.

There were many other challenges, but we overcame all of them with God's help. These situations have all helped to build character and strength in my wife and children and me, but it was not without hard work and determination.

I am not looking for sympathy from my readers. I have worked through my problems and overcome them to a point where I have abundant peace and fulfillment in my life. I have a great relationship with my mother, siblings, and beloved wife, whom I have been with for almost nineteen years. I love my wonderful, intelligent sons, who are nineteen and sixteen years old. I have forgiven all of the people who hurt me in my past and even pray for them.

My wife and I have rental property, good jobs, and because of my praying mother and the blessing of God are having positive experiences with our finances since going bankrupt. It has been a long road to rebuild our lives, but we are making progress.

So as you read this, hopefully you will be encouraged to keep trudging along to reach your goals and the goals that God has for you. There is no set protocol to reach those goals. We have an infinite God who has infinite resources to help you. Dream big and ask much of our extravagant God. He is so very generous. It would be good to incorporate a sense of humour into your journey. It will do wonders for you.

God is not interested in causing problems or hardship in our lives; that is what the devil does. But God uses those situations to make us stronger and develop us into great people. If we do not work to make that development occur, we become bitter and stagnated and do not move forward. However, if that development does occur, through us overcoming our problems, we become successful, influential people who do great things and live fulfilling lives.

The most inspirational message I can relay to you is: "Never give up…never give up…never give up." If you think that your life is over and that there is no hope for you, you are sadly mistaken. God is the great Redeemer, the giver of hope, and the God of second chances. He makes the impossible happen in the lives of those who are willing to believe and persevere.

Remember when you are in need or in crisis that we have an infinite God with infinite solutions!

1 - Starting Out

I was born in beautiful Medicine Hat, Alberta, Canada, in December of 1967. I asked my mother to give me some information about my childhood and what kind of a child I was. With laughter in her voice she talked about the times she would take me with her to go grocery shopping. She would set me in a shopping cart and have to push it down the exact centre of the aisle so that I wouldn't grab items off the shelves and put them into the cart. She also remembered that I would go into our basement and take off all of my clothes. I do not remember this, fortunately, because I was only two years old.

I do remember running away with the ice cream man one hot summer afternoon when I was around the age of four. I did not have any money, so I thought that if I followed him long enough he would get sick of me and give me some ice cream. When my parents found me my father jumped out of the car, grabbed me, and let me have it. He was not impressed, and I don't blame him. I think I was more sorry that I had not gotten any ice cream than I was for getting caught.

On Friday nights my father would play guitar at the German Harmony Club. So each Friday I would shine his dress shoes for him before he went out. He would come home from work and eat supper. Then at around 7:00 p.m. he would take off with his guitar and amplifier. Sometimes on Saturday mornings he would get up early and come downstairs to sit with me while I was watching cartoons and my brother and sister were still sleeping. He would start telling jokes to make me laugh. My father had a great sense of humour, which I inherited. It has helped me tremendously throughout my life, especially when things were most difficult.

Ever since I can remember my mother had taken my siblings and I to church. One time at Sunday School my teacher asked me if I wanted to ask Jesus into my heart. So I agreed to and went through a booklet called *The Four Spiritual Laws.* I felt so clean and pure inside. I was about eight years old. However, it would be many years before I would see the power of God and benefits of being a Christian manifest in my life.

My parents started to have serious problems when I was nine years old. I didn't pay much attention to it, because they had fought before. However, when the fighting became more frequent I started to worry. They would tell us kids to go into the living room, and after a while the screaming and yelling would start. Then the dishes would start to break, and finally they would start hitting each other. It would carry on well into the night. Sometimes I would wake up in the middle of the night and hear them fighting. As one person said, some couples fight so much the only thing they have in common is that they were married on the same day.

I remember one day when my father came home from work drunk and started to fight with my mother. Then he sat down on the stairs and cried. As soon as I saw him crying I started to cry too. I did not know why my parents were fighting so much. I did not realize that my dad had lost his job and had to declare bankruptcy. Shortly before this his father had passed away, and they were very close. My father came home drunk more and more frequently after this.

One night after supper my father came into the living room. He sat down and said, fighting back tears, "I have something to tell you kids." My sister, brother, and I all exchanged glances of bewilderment.

Dad started to speak again. This time his voice was frail and he had tears full of pain in his eyes. "Mom and I are splitting up." That was all that he said. Then he got up and left the room.

Shortly after that my father moved out. We only saw him once every couple of weeks. We also moved to another part of town. I was now a lot closer my school and no longer had to take the bus to get there. Many of my school friends lived in that area, so the move was good for me in many ways. I had six good friends whom I played with. We played hide and seek, kick the can, ball tag, and many other fun games. Sometimes we would go bike riding or catching frogs. It was a great deal of fun.

I could tell that my mother was really hurt from the divorce. I remember her saying to us kids very angrily, "Your father is not getting our phone number or anything."

I was in grade five now, and life never did seem to get boring. I played soccer on a city league, did my homework to keep a B average, and attended the First Assembly of God church every Sunday.

Grade six went by, and near the end of the year I took ill with rheumatic fever. All of the joints in my body swelled up, and every time I moved I was in pain. When I came out of the hospital I stayed home for two more weeks. I had now missed about four weeks of school, and when I went back I found it very hard to concentrate. I would sit in class and wonder, sometimes for half of the day, if I was going to pass my grade or not. I was very worried about it. Nevertheless, I did pass grade six, with a B average.

At night the pain was so bad that I could not sleep. Sometimes my mom would come and pray for me while I tried to sleep on the floor in the living room. Other times she would get upset and tell me to be quiet so that she could sleep. Twice a week my mother walked with me to the hospital so that I could get physiotherapy for my joints. I would sit in a tub full of water and be instructed by a physiotherapist to do exercises for about half an hour. It was very painful to do the exercises, and progress was slow.

When I was in the hospital I encountered other kids who had chronic kidney problems, cancer, and other health issues. As I look back I realize that my short illness was trivial compared to the lifelong challenges they faced. I am so thankful that I got better through exercise and hard work. Those children could do very little to change their circumstances.

At home, life was always a challenge. We were well below the poverty line, and my mother had to take care of my younger sister, older brother, and myself. My father was not around very much, because he was always working. I remember phoning over to his apartment at night, and he would often answer the phone drunk. This caused our conversations to be limited and cut short. My mother was having a lot of problems with money, taking care of her three kids, and her relationship with our father. When I asked her to play a game or spend time with me, she would always decline. She would make excuses like "I'm too tired," or "I don't feel like it right now."

I believe that she was emotionally unavailable for me due to the fact that she was dealing with so much financial stress and other problems. This lack of attention started to really affect me. I wanted some attention but was not getting any from my mom or dad.

Having parents who did not spend much time with me has greatly motivated me to be a better parent with my own children. I wanted to make sure that I took time for my kids. I have two wonderful sons, who I did all sorts of things with when they were growing up. We would have water balloon fights, catch frogs, go fishing, play sports together, and do many other activities together. Many bad things that happened in my life have become great strengths for me as I used them for my gain. I have countless examples of this in my life.

Because of the lack of attention, I started going to the arcades and hanging out. I would go and play pinball or shoot pool. But this required money. I had a job at the townhouses where we lived before we moved. Once a week I would ride my bike there, remove all of the garbage cans from their stalls, and sweep up the garbage on the ground. I received ten dollars a week for this.

I started to spend more and more time and money at the arcade. Soon my money ran out, but I wanted to play more pinball. At home money was always in short supply. We were on social assistance, so my mother never had any money to give us. So I started stealing from friends and family members. Sometimes I would look for pop bottles and cash them in. In the winter I would shovel driveways for money, and in the summer I would rake leaves. I became very resourceful in order to reach some of my financial goals.

Gradually my relationship with my mother grew weaker and we grew farther apart emotionally. I became angry at her for rejecting me all of the time. My anger grew into a deep-seated rage. I had become sort of a loner. I had friends that I hung around with, but it was mostly at the arcades.

School started in the fall again, and I was now in grade seven. But something had changed in me. I no longer had the drive to get good marks, partly because of getting sick and not doing a lot of work while being laid up and partly because of the lack of support at home. My mother had taken a full-time job at the Hudson's Bay store and was around home even less than before. Once someone asked me what I wanted to be when I got out of high school and I said, "Hopefully under twenty-two years old."

I had started to smoke before grade seven began. I quit doing my homework and started smoking even more. I began arguing with my mother constantly. I never wanted to be around my home or around her. I was becoming the kind of person that my mother didn't want me hanging around with. My whole life was just a bad habit.

About once every month my father would have my brother, sister, and me over to his place for a barbecue. He would pick us up and spend the day with us. I really enjoyed the time with him. We would listen to music and visit while he cooked. It gave my mother a break too. My brother was now fourteen, and he was working out on the pipeline in the summer with my father. When school started he worked there on the weekends.

Report card time rolled around, and I knew my marks were going to be bad. I had not done any work at school at all. I ended up with a very low average. When my mother saw my report card she was very upset. She lectured me, yelled, and threatened. To me it was just another shouting match, and I didn't let it affect me. I just kept on smoking, stealing, and playing pinball. I hated school, and I seldom studied or even looked at my books.

In December one of my school friends approached me about taking over his early morning paper route. It involved getting up at six in the morning and delivering about thirty papers. Enthusiastically I accepted his offer. I talked it over with my mom, and she said I had better wait to see what my father said about it.

I talked it over with my dad, and he said it was okay, but if my marks dropped any farther then I would have to quit the job. I think at this point if my marks had dropped any farther they would have been below zero.

My mother had to get up at six every morning to wake me up except for Saturday. But that was the day my brother went to work, so she had to get up and wake him up. She never got to sleep in.

When I delivered papers in the morning I would try to beat the milkman to some of the houses so that I could steal the money put out for the milk. I would take it and buy cigarettes with it. It's a good thing that I did not live in New York or I probably would have become involved with the mob.

A month before Christmas I had started telling my mother that I wanted a small pinball game. Christmas eventually came, and I woke up early and made my way downstairs to the tree with my brother and sister. We were looking at the presents to see which ones had our names on them. We had sort of a tradition for opening presents. We would open one present before breakfast and then open the rest after we ate.

We all ate as fast as we could and then went over to the tree and started opening our presents. I finished opening all of my presents, and I did not get the pinball game. "Why didn't you get me that game I wanted?" I asked my mother angrily. "You never buy me what I want!" Then I stormed out of the house, slamming the door behind me. This must have broken her heart. I can't imagine how hard it must have been to come up with enough money to even buy us presents for Christmas. I came back into the house later on and apologized for the way I had acted.

The Christmas holidays came and went. Report card time came along again, and somehow some of my marks had come up a bit. Everyone knows that I did not bribe the teachers with free coffee either, because Tim Horton's had not yet been built. However, my marks were not high enough to give me passing grades. Before I arrived home I decided to change my marks. I changed the number 2 on the 20 percent to a 7 so that it looked like 70 percent. I also changed the 3 on the 30 percent to an 8 so that it looked like 80 percent. I had creative talent, but I was using it for the wrong purposes.

I left my report card on the stairs at home and rode my bike to where I had to work. As I rode down the street, a car drove past me with a handbag on top of it. "Maybe there's money in it," I told myself. I followed the car, and the driver walked into a house without noticing the bag on top of the vehicle. Very methodically I crept over to the car and slid the handbag into my arms. Then I ducked low as I made my way back behind some bushes. I took the wallet out and threw the bag into the garbage. I moved to a safe place out of sight of anyone and opened the wallet. There was twenty-two dollars in it. I scooped it into my pocket and threw the wallet into a garbage can. I then did my work and rode my bike home.

When I got home my mother was already looking at my report card. "Boy, you sure got good marks, Greg," she stated, very pleased.

I was proud of myself too. Everything was going good. I had money and good grades, and my mom was not bugging me about school. But my good fortune did not last very long. A concerned teacher phoned my mother and warned her to push me more in the area of my homework. I was outside when my mother called me. "You get into this house right now! You're grounded!"

Now I had to figure out if she was mad at me because she had found out I had stolen some money or that I had altered the marks on my report card. I am surprised that I did not give myself a coronary by the time I was thirteen due to the stress I put on myself.

"How could you lie to me and change your marks?" my mother asked with tears in her eyes. "Wasn't the 10 or 15 percent increase in your average enough? I would have been pleased with you still."

I did not believe her. I did not know what would please her. I barely even knew my mother. I never spent any time with her. It seemed that whenever I was home (which was almost never), my mother was out having coffee with someone. If my mother was home, I was out playing pinball or stealing money for pinball.

2 - Growing Trouble

I kept stealing more and more to feed my growing appetite for pinball, cigarettes, and the occasional joint of marijuana. I had been introduced to drugs by an acquaintance at school. It's a good thing I was not born in Las Vegas or I probably would have been gambling too.

One night I was walking around outside looking for something to steal, and I spotted a chequebook in a car. Quickly I opened the car door, grabbed the chequebook, and took off.

The next day I came home at lunchtime from school and wrote out a cheque for fifty dollars. Then I took it to the drugstore and cashed it. *Man, is this easy money!* I thought as I walked toward the arcade. I bought a pack of smokes and got some quarters for the games.

A few days later when I ran out of money I wrote out another cheque, for forty dollars, and took it to the drugstore again. I am positive that I put at least three arcade owners' kids through college.

"How come your last name is different from before?" the cashier asked. The same cashier had cashed the first cheque too.

"Oh, my parents are getting a divorce, and I used my mom's last name this time instead of my father's," I lied confidently.

"Oh, I see," she said with an understanding voice. Then she punched some buttons and produced forty dollars for me. I left, smiling and thanking her as I put the money in my pocket. Then to the arcade I went.

Because of my increased absence from school my mother phoned Social Services. She set up an appointment for me with a counsellor. So I rode my bike to his office and waited for quite a while until finally a man approached me and stuck out his hand.

"Hi, I'm Greg, " he said with a friendly, warm smile.

What a cool first name he has, I thought. "My name is Greg," I replied coldly.

We sat down in his office, and I listened impatiently while he explained that he was going to try to help me expand my interests and direct my mind to other areas of recreation besides pinball, smoking, and drinking. Perhaps he was my addiction counsellor and I just did not know it at that point.

He asked me how school was going and how my marks were. I gave him one-word answers. "Fine." "Okay." "Good." I was still in denial at this point. We talked for about half an hour, and I said very little. *What's this guy butting into my life for anyway?* I thought. *Why is he asking me so many questions, and how does he know so much about me?* I wondered angrily.

At this point in my life I did not have many friends. I was very much a loner. The only thing I still did with other kids was play soccer on a team in the city league. I loved to play soccer and could still run well in spite of being a smoker. At school I was quiet and kept to myself. A lot of the other kids picked on me, perhaps because I was very defensive and would overreact. I always said the wrong thing and ended up making people hate me more and more. I soon became the object of their teasing and ridicule. This caused me to want to be away from school even more. At least I was not prejudiced; I seemed to have a way of getting everyone to hate me.

I remember telling my mother that a bunch of the kids at school were always making fun of me, and she did nothing to help me. I think she didn't realize how serious it was. She didn't have the resources to help me or to suggest what I could do to improve things at school.

The anger inside of me grew and grew. I would walk around at school and home hating everyone in sight. It's no wonder I didn't have any friends. I didn't want any friends anyway. I just wanted to play pinball and smoke.

I started going to pools, hotels, and other public places that I thought would be an easy score for money. I would wait until there was nobody left in the change rooms and then I would search through people's jeans for money. But the day came when my stealing caught up with me.

I had been skipping school and was playing pool at the arcade when my father pulled up in his truck. I walked outside the arcade very slowly. I feared that my father had found something out and that I was going to get into trouble. My heart pounded rapidly as I neared his truck. By the look on his face I could tell that he was not impressed.

"Get into the truck," he barked.

I was hoping that we were going to go somewhere for coffee to talk about what was bothering him, but it did not turn out that way. He drove me to my house, which was four blocks away, took me into my room, and pulled the belt off of his pants. Then he started hitting me with it. I jumped all over the room trying to avoid his swinging. This was clearly motivation to enrol in gymnastics so that I could get better at dodging my father.

"No, Dad, I won't do it again! I'm sorry! Please don't hit

me," I begged as I further tried to dodge his hits.

He threw me onto the bed and cocked his fist back, ready to hit me in the face.

"Oh, I could just drive you one," he threatened through clenched teeth. "Why weren't you in school today?"

There was a long silence before I started to speak. Then tears formed in my eyes. My voice cracked, "I don't have any friends at school. I go to school and everyone makes fun of me," I pleaded.

"You have friends at school," my father stated confidently, "You just don't know who they are." But my father had never gone over to my school or even been in my classroom.

"There's something else that I found out today. You stole a bunch of money from Grandma and her neighbour," he said in a matter-of-fact voice. "What did you do with all of that money, spend it on drugs?"

I did not reply.

"C'mon. We're going for a drive," he ordered.

We jumped into his truck and drove to my grandmother's house. We knocked on the door and walked into the house. Dad made me face her and apologize to her. Then he took me next door and made me apologize to her neighbour as well.

Dad then drove me home and talked to my mother privately. I ended up being grounded for a week after that.

I still had the chequebook I had stolen and decided to write out another cheque. This time it was for eighty dollars. I walked to a bank downtown and approached the teller. A friend of mine, Kevin, accompanied me. We were going to go play pinball after we got some money.

"Hi. I would like to cash this cheque," I stated confidently as I looked at the teller with a phoney smile.

The teller looked at the cheque and asked, "Did your mother write this cheque for you?"

"Yes," I lied, starting to feel uneasy.

"Okay, well, I'm going to call her and talk with her for a minute," she replied calmly.

I knew something was wrong, and my heart started to race along with my mind. The bank teller reappeared and said, "If you want to come with me I'll show you where you can wait." She showed us to a room in the back and told us to wait there until my supposed mother arrived.

I was very nervous and uneasy as I waited for an accuser to confront me and tell me that I was not her son. My eyes were carefully probing the room as I tried to think of a way to get out of there without being caught. Then I suddenly had an idea. I motioned for Kevin to come with me as I walked out to where the bank teller was standing.

"Hi. We're just going to go lock up our bikes and we'll be right back," I lied nervously. I was thankful that my nose did not get longer when I spoke those words to her. We walked outside and took off running as fast as we could.

"We'd better go home, Greg," Kevin stated. "I don't want to be picked up by the police!"

"Forget it, Kevin, and quit worrying," I reassured him. "The cops aren't going to look for us. Now let's go and play some pinball."

Two minutes later we were walking down the street toward the arcade, and cops pulled up beside us in an unmarked car. The bank teller was in the car too. I saw a finger through the window motioning for us to come toward the car. It was a police officer.

"Come here, you guys," the cop ordered us. "Get in the car!"

The policeman took us down to the station and put us in

separate rooms and then questioned us. Then he phoned my mother, and she came down to the police station. He asked if I knew anything about the two other cheques that had been written, forged, and cashed.

"Nope," I lied. "I know nothing about them."

"We're going to look into this and find out who did forge these other cheques," he stated emphatically.

My mother, looked upset once she was informed by the officer what I had done. Then he gave us both a ride home.

The next day when I woke up I did not have to go to school because a police officer was coming over to talk to me about the other two cheques. He had both cheques in his hand as he knocked on our door and then came in.

"Is this your handwriting?" he asked.

"No," I lied.

"Well, write down a sentence with this pen and I'll see if the writing matches," he ordered me.

I should have lied and told him that I couldn't spell or said, "Just look at my report card and you will see my English marks." I started to write on the paper. The officer picked up the paper and held it to the cheque to see if the writing was similar.

"Well, it sure looks like your handwriting matches this cheque," he said.

I started to make up some lies to defend myself, but they were very poor ones, and the officer did not buy them. "Come on," he said sarcastically, "you can do better than that." Then he charged me and told me that I would be summoned to court in the near future.

A few days later I received a piece of paper stating that I had to appear in court exactly one week from that day. I was rattled at the thought of going to court.

3 - The Break-In

A few days went by, and after everyone cooled down I decided to get myself some money. If I had worked as hard at school as I did at stealing money I would have been a rocket scientist by grade 10. I still had my paper route, and so I phoned one of my customers to see if she would be home that night so that I could collect from her. My plan was that if she was not going to be home I would break into her home and get some money.

"Hello, this is Greg. I was wondering if you were going to be home tonight because I want to collect the money for the papers," I lied.

"No, I'm sorry, we will be out tonight. Can you come tomorrow?" the woman asked.

"Yeah, I guess that will be okay," I replied. *Perfect,* I thought. *I'll just cruise over there tonight and get myself some cash.*

I phoned a buddy of mine to see if he wanted to come and help me break into the house. "C'mon, Dean," I conned him. "All you have to do is keep watch and if a car comes just yell to me."

"Yeah, I guess I could do that," he responded, giving in to my request.

We went to the house at about 7 p.m. I brought a screwdriver with me. The lights were off and the car was gone, so

I figured we had a little time to do this. I started taking the frame off the mail slot in the door, because I was hoping I would be able to reach through and around and open the door once it was off. I tried, but my arms were too short.

Next I tried taking off the patio door, but I was also not successful at this. I looked over at Dean nervously, and he shook his head at me to signal no cars were coming. I walked all the way around the house looking for a way in but could not find any.

"Hey," Dean whispered loudly, "somebody is coming."

I took off toward the trees where Dean was, and we both watched nervously as a car pulled up into the driveway. It was the owners of the house. The frame of the mail slot was hanging from the door. Dean and I both ran, panicked as could be. We parted company and I went home, trying not to act suspicious as I walked into the house.

The next morning a cop car pulled up to my house and an officer knocked at the door. "Oh no," I said to myself, "not again."

"Hi, Greg," the officer greeted me cheerfully. "I know I said I would see you later, but I didn't think it would be this quick." Well, at least the officer was in a good mood and happy to see me. If I had a daily planner at this point I would have checked it to see if it said, "Run and hide."

He started to ask me questions about where I was the night before, what I had been doing, and who I was with. Every question he asked I answered with a lie.

"A house that was broken into last night, and you had phoned the lady of this house last night to see if she would be home or not," he said in a matter-of-fact way. "There were footprints in the snow at her house from winter boots. Bring me one of your boots, please."

Slowly and fearfully I went and got one of my boots for him. As I look back now I realize I should have told him that we were so poor that I had a timeshare on my winter boots and the other guy had them that week. *He's gonna know it was me,* I worried to myself.

He carefully examined the boot. My heart was pounding in overdrive as I watched for his reaction. After a long pause he looked up at me and spoke. "Yup, I bet if I measured the footprints in the snow they would match this boot perfectly," he said confidently.

I was speechless. I could not say a thing to defend myself. I did not dare look at my mother, because I did not want to see her reaction to my latest escapade.

Disgusted and frustrated beyond words, my mother sent me to school. I was nervous all day. I was wearing out what little trust everyone still had in me.

A few days later I woke up and knew it was the day I had to go to court. I started to get dressed while my brother and sister got ready for school. My father drove up to our house in his truck. He was going to drive us to the courthouse.

"Well, are you ready to get this over with?" my father asked.

"Yeah, I…I guess so," I replied. In my mind I wanted to run away and never come back. I wished I had never gotten myself into the mess I was in. I wished that someone had told me how to stop doing what I was doing wrong.

This was the first time I ever had to go to court, and I did not know what to expect. It was very icy as we drove down a steep hill to the courthouse. We fishtailed back and forth down the hill. *Great! Maybe we will crash and then I won't have to go,* I desperately hoped.

Unfortunately, we made it to court. Nervously I waited outside the courtroom for my name to be called. Fifteen minutes later we went in.

"All rise," a voice commanded us. Everyone stood up as a guy dressed in black entered the room. It was the judge.

Where's his hammer and curly hair? I wondered to myself, trying to make the best of a bad situation with humour. *Maybe he'll order everyone to just calm down and forget about my incidents.*

Everyone sat down as soon as the judge did. Then he took a piece of paper out of a folder and carefully started to read it. I looked around the room nervously. I saw a lady typing feverishly and about fifteen other people I did not know.

What are all of these people doing here? I thought. *You know, this would be a good time to play "Simon Says," because everyone is so quiet and there's only one guy facing us while the rest are facing him.*

Suddenly my wandering thoughts were snapped back to reality. "Please stand up," the judge ordered me quietly. "Are you Gregory Todd Van Riper?"

Yeah, but I plan on changing my name, I thought. Scared, I stood up as I looked to my parents for some support, and then I faced the judge. "Yes," I whispered.

"Did you steal, forge, and cash these cheques for money?" he asked.

"Yes," I replied as my heart beat rapidly in my chest.

Then the judge went through the same process for the house I had broken into.

"I recommend twelve months of probation," the judge finally announced.

That's it, I thought with relief. *Probation! No sweat, man.* I left the courtroom with my parents, and my father drove me to school and said goodbye.

Time went by, and I kept stealing from people. However, I was much more selective about where I stole from.

One night I had to go to a soccer game and needed a ride. I rode my bike over to my friend's house. I rang the doorbell, and his mother opened the door and asked me to come in.

"I'm down here," Bruce called to me.

I walked into a room, but it was the wrong one. I had never been to his house before.

"No, over here," he shouted again.

"Okay," I replied. But something had caught my eye. There was a wad of bills on the dresser in a sour cream container. I walked out of the room toward Bruce's voice.

"Are you ready for the game tonight?" he asked.

"You bet, man! We're gonna kill 'em," I replied, trying to show the same amount of enthusiasm.

We rode up to the field and started to warm up. But all through the game I kept thinking about the money I had seen. *Man, there must have been about fifty bucks in there!*

We went back to his house after the game, and I asked him if I could use the bathroom. "Sure," he replied. "It's downstairs."

I ran down the stairs into the room where I had seen the money. I grabbed the wad and stuck it into my pocket. With my hand inside of the same pocket, guarding the money from being seen, I headed to the bathroom. But Bruce saw me walking away from the room I had taken the money from.

"Where were you?" he asked.

I didn't know what to say, but the gears were grinding awfully hard to think of an excuse. "I think I've got diarrhea," I lied.

Then Bruce watched me as I walked into the bathroom. I panicked. *What should I do? Where will I hide this money? What if I get caught? I wish I had not come back down here, because I'm gonna get caught now. All of the kids at school will know about it,* I told myself, tormented.

My heart was pounding hard. Finally I got an idea. I laid the money out flat and tucked it into my shorts. Then I tucked my shirt into my shorts and checked myself in the mirror to see if anything looked suspicious. Then I flushed the toilet and walked out of the bathroom.

Bruce was waiting for me with doubt and suspicion all over his face. "What were you doing in that room?" he asked.

"I couldn't find the bathroom. I thought it was over there," I lied nervously.

Then Bruce started to frisk my pockets. "What's this?" he asked as he pulled two dollars out of my pocket.

I took the two dollars and said, "It's mine. I got it to buy a pop and chocolate bar after the game."

After the confrontation I walked up the stairs, said goodbye, and left quickly. I did not want to be searched any more. I was already sweating bullets.

I rode my bike home, but before I walked into the house my brother came outside and asked, "How much money do you have?"

"A couple of dollars," I lied.

"You do not," my brother said. "You have eighty-seven dollars that you stole from Bruce's sister!"

"What are you talking about?" I challenged back, playing dumb.

He did not reply, so I walked past him into the house and went up to the room I shared with him. I pulled the money out and stuck it into my pillowcase. My mother was out somewhere having coffee or visiting with someone. I changed my clothes and then took five dollars and went down to the arcade to play pinball. I lit up a cigarette and tried to relax, but I knew I would be hearing more about this the next day.

When I arrived home my mother started to question me. She asked me if I had taken the money, and I said no. Every question she asked me I answered with a lie. I was a chronic liar. If someone had asked me what my name was, I probably would have lied to them.

After a few more questions I went to bed. I never had any trouble sleeping, either. But I did not realize that my conscience did not bother me any more because it had been numbed by me doing so many bad things. I had lied to and stolen from so many people and had done so many bad things to support my habits that I did not care any more about how much I was hurting other people.

The next day I woke up and immediately thought about what I had done the night before. I cringed at the thought of everyone at school bugging me and making fun of me. Nevertheless, I went to school. By the time I arrived everyone had already heard about what had happened the night before. One of Bruce's friends came up to me and said, "You're in big trouble." I felt like a politician after a sex scandal.

I just looked at him with a hateful stare.

When I got to my first class everybody started to bug me and call me names. They were doing the job that my conscience could no longer do. I put up with them for about half an hour and then walked out of the classroom. We were in the middle of our industrial arts class, so luckily I was able to get up and leave without any of the teachers interrogating me as to where I was going.

I skipped out of school for the rest of the day and rode my bike around town, spending the money I had stolen. "What a bunch of jerks. I'll get even with them," I promised myself.

I came home from school at about four o'clock. By now my mother was home from work. A few minutes later the phone rang. It was the principal of my school. He informed my mother that I had been away from school all day. She turned and looked at me with shock and disgust. I could tell that it was going to be bad. She hung up the phone and told me that I had been dismissed from school for the rest of the year. "You're really smart!" she scolded me angrily.

I did not even care. "Big deal," I told myself carelessly. "I hate school anyway. Nobody understands me or even cares about me."

That same night the police phoned my mother and told her that they wanted to talk with me the next morning. It was about the money that had been taken from Bruce's place. I was dreading seeing them and did not want to go through with another question-and-answer period.

In the morning they showed up at 8:30 like they had said they would.

"Look," the cop said bluntly, "I'm going to ask you if you took the money. If you lie, I'll make sure that you go to a place where you are locked up all of the time. It's going to be a nice summer, and you will not want to be there. But if you tell the truth, you might get off with probation. Did you steal the money?"

"No," I lied coldly.

"Look, man, it's going to be a nice summer, and you won't want to be locked up," he repeated.

"Yeah, you just want me to say that I took the money, even

if I didn't," I said defensively. Then I got up and walked into the bathroom and locked the door. I knew that the cop knew I was guilty.

"Get out of there," my mother ordered me sharply.

As I walked out of the bathroom I heard the officer say, "I think we better take him to YAC." YAC is an acronym for Youth Assessment Centre, a place where young delinquents are taken to await court cases or to serve time for crimes that they have committed.

"All right, you go ahead and take him then," my mother consented. "I'll go and pack his clothes."

Tears started to form in my eyes, and with desperation I said, "Okay, I did steal the money. I took it; just don't send me away."

"It's too late for that. You had your chance to tell the truth," the officer said, almost seeming to enjoy my desperation.

I turned around and bolted out the door, down the steps and out into the yard. I ran down the back alley with the officer following me. While I ran I had tears in my eyes. I ran through another yard and back into my house. I did not know where else to run. I wanted my mother to defend me from the officer taking me away, but she did not. It seemed like she wanted a break from me and all of my problems that caused her more grief. Maybe everyone needed to look at the reason why I was behaving so badly all of the time. Perhaps I needed more attention from my parents, and the only way I could get it was by being bad.

My mother had packed a suitcase for me. She phoned my father at work and let him know that I was being taken to YAC. My father seemed indifferent and did nothing to keep them from taking me away either. *Doesn't anybody want me?* I thought angrily.

The cop grabbed my suitcase and said, "Well, I guess we're on our way."

I grabbed my mother in great desperation, hugging her, holding on to her, and crying, "Mom, please don't let him take me. Don't let me go, Mom! I won't steal any more; just don't let him take me, Mom," I pleaded.

"They're going to try and help you, honey," my mother replied softly.

I remember following the officer to his car and getting in. He drove me to YAC, and as we drove I cried hot tears of anger for the rejection I was feeling. I was scared, angry, and confused. Why did my mother not stick up for me and hold on to me? She could have done something to try and help me. I felt so unloved and unwanted by everyone.

As I look back I realize that there were many people who loved me very much. But my poor behaviour distanced me from them considerably. My inconsideration and divisive tendencies could not be tolerated by those closest to me, because they could not trust me. Over the years my examination of my poor behaviour from the past has been a fantastic stepping stone to improving my life. It was almost like a mirror to look into to see what was wrong in order to know what I had to fix so that I would not be so destructive and abrasive to other people. It has worked in my favour, galvanizing me to become a better person. I know how to establish and maintain loving relationships with others. I have many friends at this point in my life whom I have known for years.

4 - Sent Away

I did not know what to expect from the place I was going to. We drove up to a large one-storey building. The cop stepped up to the door and rang a buzzer. A guy opened the door, and we walked into the main centre. As I walked in I saw a group of kids sitting on a couch. I was told to sit with them and wait. So I started to talk with one of the kids. I was twelve years old, and he was older, a teenager.

"Where ya going?" I asked him quietly.

"Camping," he replied.

"Oh, sounds like fun," I replied.

Then a man came over to me and said, "C'mon, we're going in there." He pointed to a room and told me to strip and turn on the shower.

"Ya scared?" he asked me calmly. I nodded my head as I started to take my shower.

"Do you smoke?" he asked.

"No," I lied. I did not want him to know that I smoked in case he was going to tell my mother. As if she did not already know. After I got dressed, he showed me around the centre. He showed me my bedroom, the kitchen, the schoolroom, the washroom, and finally the recreation room. In the recreation room was a pool table, a Ping-Pong table, a stereo, and a television. The X-box had not yet been invented. Bill Gates, where were you when I needed you?

After the tour I was given permission to play pool. "We don't know how long you are going to be staying here, so we won't put you into school until we know," one of the staff members told me.

That suits me fine, I thought. *I just want to continue playing pool and not going to school like I did before anyway.*

I received a summons a few days later telling me that I had to appear in court again. The next few days went by very slowly. But I kept busy by playing pool and listening to music.

A day at YAC consisted of getting up at about 7:30 in the morning and doing some light chores, like vacuuming or cleaning a bathroom. We would eat breakfast and then the other kids would go to school while I played pool. Then at noon we would eat lunch and they would have a cigarette break. The other kids would go back to school until about 3:30 while I played pool. After school was finished the kids would all go to their rooms for quiet hour. During this time the staff would change shifts and write out reports of the kids' behaviour or if they had an incident with one of the kids.

After quiet hour we would be free to play pool or listen to music until supper was ready. After supper we would be free to play pool until 8:00 and then have a snack and be in our rooms by 9:00 p.m.

When I played pool alone I would think a lot. I wondered where I had gone wrong in my life. How did I get into this mess? Why did I steal all of the time? Where did all of my friends go that I had in grade 6? On and on I thought about my life as I shot pool. Why did our family turn out the way it did?

Every time I went to bed I cried. I was lonely and confused about why I was in this place, why I had been taken away from my home, and why nobody would help me. I prayed to God and promised "God, if you get me out of here I'll never steal again." Then I cried myself to sleep.

By the end of the week I was sick of life at YAC. Everywhere I went I had to be followed by a staff member. He would unlock the door before I went through it and then lock it after I was through the door. It was like they had total control of me.

Finally I snapped one day. "I'm sick of this place and I want to leave. Just get me out of here!" I screamed.

"You'll have to calm down," a staff worker told me calmly. "After your court case you may have to spend some time in here. Why don't you go and play pool for a while?" she suggested.

"I don't want to play pool," I screamed. "I want to leave!"

When my court day came, the police escorted me to the court house. We walked into the courthouse and I met my mother there. Then we were called into the courtroom.

"All rise," I heard a voice say. Then the judge walked into the room and we all sat down.

Everything happened like it did before, only this time four offences were read off instead of two. There was also a man in the room who started to talk about me openly to everyone. "He skips out of school, he steals, he lies to the authorities, and he smokes," he stated harshly.

Hey, someone shut that guy up, I thought.

Then the judge said in a blunt voice, "I recommend six months in the Lethbridge Sifton Children's Centre."

Six months, I told myself in disbelief. *That means that I have to leave Medicine Hat and won't be with my family.*

The instant that we stepped out of the courtroom I started to cry. "Six months," I sobbed to my mother, "not *six months.*"

"They're going to try to help you, honey," my mother said compassionately as she tried to console me.

Then an officer escorted me back to YAC. I was then ordered to pack my things because I would be going back home for a week before being sent to Lethbridge. About an hour later my social worker picked me up and took me to a foster home for the remainder of the day so that I would be supervised until my father picked me up after work to take me home.

I got out of the car and walked into the house with my gym bag full of clothes. A woman greeted me with a friendly smile. She was older, about five feet tall, with blonde hair. I was shown to the living room, where I was allowed to watch television or read. I said goodbye to the social worker and started to watch television.

After about ten minutes I was bored and I wanted a cigarette. I asked the woman if there was something else that I could do.

"No," she snapped impatiently, "you just sit and watch television until your father comes to pick you up."

Oh, that's really open-minded of her, I thought.

The only thing on television at 2 in the afternoon is soap operas. What was I supposed to do, sit on the couch and cry because Rachael was leaving Tom?

After talking with me for two minutes the woman realized that I was very mouthy. "No wonder you're in so much trouble all of the time, you have such a sharp tongue," she informed me.

I thought, *I don't have to take this garbage from her. I'm gonna take off out of here.*

I placed my gym bag beside me, and as soon as she went into the kitchen I took off out the front door and caught a bus up to my house. I got home and lit up a cigarette. I went into the house a few minutes later, and the phone rang.

"Oh no, it's the cops!" I picked up the phone hesitantly. "Hello?" I said.

"Hi, Greg, you're home, eh?" my father asked.

"Yeah," I replied, a bit more at ease after finding out he wasn't angry with me for running away. "I got sick of sitting around there so I came home."

"Well, stay at home until your mother gets there, okay?" he asked politely.

"Yeah, sure, Dad. There's nowhere for me to go anyway," I reassured him.

The day came when my social worker picked me up. My father had come by to see me off since both of my parents did not know when they would see me again. I hugged them both before getting into the car. I waived goodbye and prepared myself for the trip ahead of me.

Lethbridge was about a two-hour drive from Medicine Hat. "It's just going to be like going on a long vacation," I said, trying to comfort myself.

I did not say much to the social worker on the way there though. I thought, *Man, too bad you didn't tell the truth to that cop. You could be at the pool hall right now playing a game of pinball and having a smoke.* I could have been honing my bad habits.

We arrived in Lethbridge and pulled up to a large one-storey building. It was about twice the size of YAC. It also had a large backyard covered with grass and a few bushes here and there. "No more locked doors," my social worker told me, trying to make me feel better. I stepped out of the car into my new home.

I was introduced to some of the staff workers. They asked me a whole bunch of personal questions about myself. They weighed me and took my height too. Then they showed me around the building and introduced me to some of the other kids. They explained some of the rules to me and showed me where I would be sleeping. I had to share a room with three other kids. Boys were on one side of the building and girls were on the other. The age range was from about seven to fourteen. One of the girls who had been at YAC was now also at the centre in Lethbridge. Her name was Cindy. She greeted me with a smile. It was good to see at least one familiar face from Medicine Hat.

I asked the staff if I was allowed to smoke, and they said I was not. *This could be a problem,* I told myself with frustration. *Nobody can expect me to quit all of my bad habits at once, can they?*

We ate supper, then cleared off the table and watched television for a while. It was now around the middle of May in 1980. School was almost out for the year, but I was ordered to go to school anyway. School classes were held inside the centre. I was given grade 7 work to do and did it very well. I was a smart kid but just did not want to apply myself. What if I used up all of my brain power now and had none left for later on in my life?

The daily schedule was almost a carbon copy of YAC, with the exception of the locked doors. On weekends we would play sports or go out and have a picnic. Sometimes on a school night one of the staff would take us swimming or to the store to get a drink of pop.

A few weeks went by, and I was starting to get bored with

the daily routine. Scott, a Native Canadian, and I took off from the centre one morning. We went outside, jumped the fence, and ran across a main street into a cluster of houses. We walked downtown, only a few blocks away, and went into a mall. We walked around in the mall for a while and just looked around. After stealing some cigarettes we left the mall and walked around town for a while.

We came to a schoolyard and stole a couple of bikes to ride around on. I told Scott that I felt like riding to Medicine Hat. So we started to pedal toward my hometown. We rode for hours and hours. In every town that we came to we found better bikes than the ones we were riding on. So we would leave the old bikes and take the better bikes.

By 10:30 that night we had made it to Bow Island, about 30 miles from Medicine Hat. We had pedalled about 100 miles that day. It started to rain, so we looked for some temporary shelter. We did not have to look very hard though. As we rode past a house an older man stepped out of his door and asked us if we wanted to come inside for a few minutes to warm up. I looked at Scott cautiously. We were reading each other's minds as we both looked at the man hesitantly.

"Yeah, okay," I finally answered, "for a little while."

The man let us in, and his wife greeted us with a friendly voice. Then she gave us some hot chocolate.

"Where are you kids going?" the woman asked curiously.

"To Medicine Hat," I replied quickly, letting Scott know that I would do the talking.

"What are you doing out this late?"

"Well, we started riding this morning but we didn't think that it would take this long to get to where we are going," I replied, trying to sound like an adult.

After a few minutes we both finished our drinks and

started to get anxious to leave. "I think I'm going to go check on my bike and lock it up," I announced to everyone.

Scott read my mind and knew I wanted to leave, so he came with me. We grabbed our stolen bikes and took off toward Medicine Hat, lighting up cigarettes as we went. We agreed that we thought they were going to call the police on us.

We rode for another fifteen minutes. Suddenly a truck that was going the opposite direction slowed right down and hung a U-turn. I got scared and thought that it was coming after us, so I told Scott to turn around and ride the other way. I had heard stories of people getting kidnapped, and I had become fearful that we were next. As the truck sped past us it did not stop or turn back around. I told Scott to turn around again and go the other way.

As we rode our bikes down the highway we started to become fearful that the police were going to come driving down the highway after us and pick us up. So every time we saw a car coming, we got off our bikes, jumped into the ditch, and stayed low until the car passed us. After doing this for about half an hour I started to get fed up with it, so we just stayed on our bikes and pedalled. Right after our decision to do this, the very next vehicle was an RCMP car. He pulled up beside Scott and put his lights on. I kept on riding, and then heard him call to me.

I rode over to his car, and the officer said, "Let me see your left hand."

I stuck out my left hand and he looked to see if there was a scar on it. The Lethbridge centre had looked at my body for scars to identify me in situations like this one. The officer put us into the back of his car and radioed to the dispatcher at his station, informing him that he had picked up two juveniles. He was very kind to both of us as he explained that he had gotten a call to come and look for us. He had been out searching for us for quite a while and was on his way back to Medicine Hat when he spotted us on the highway.

I don't even care what happens now, I told myself bitterly, having lost all hope of making it to Medicine Hat. I was cold, tired, hungry, and wet from the rain. I felt kind of like a drowned rat in the sewer. Incidentally, my legs were not even sore the next day from all of the biking we had done.

The officer took us to a convenience store to buy us both pop and a chocolate bar. Then we got into his car and started to drive back to Lethbridge. About halfway to Lethbridge we were transferred to another RCMP car. I guess it was so that one officer did not have to drive all the way there and back to Medicine Hat.

We were almost to Lethbridge when a truck coming from the opposite direction swerved into our lane, almost hitting us. One officer looked at the other and said, "Aw, let's just get the kids to the centre."

His suggestion came too late, though, because the other officer was already turning around. "Not on your life," he replied. "That guy almost smoked us!"

Scott and I looked at each other with smiles as the RCMP turned his lights on and sped after the truck. The truck pulled over, and the woman driving it was very drunk. We could hear her talking with the officers. In the meantime another car had been called to come get us, and a short time later we were back at Sifton.

Aw, I want to see the cop shoot someone, I thought with disappointment.

When we arrived at Sifton we were searched and then told to take showers.

5 - On My Own

The next day I woke up and after eating breakfast was sent back to school. Everything returned to normal after a few days. However, a week went by, and before I had even built up any trust Scott and I ran away again. This time we headed straight for the bus depot and bought two tickets. We boarded the bus to Medicine Hat after getting some cigarettes.

We arrived in Medicine Hat at about 6:30 p.m. We grabbed something to eat and then went over to a trailer park. It was summertime, so it was quite warm outside. We stayed there quite a while. After it got dark we walked around and stole some beer from a campsite. We ended up throwing it away because we didn't like the taste of it.

Directly across from the campground was a graveyard. Scott and I decided to go there and spend the night. We did not think that the police would look for us there. We stayed in a small chapel all night long.

I thought about a joke my father had told me when we were driving past a graveyard. He asked me how many dead people I thought were there. I said that I did not know. Then he said that they were all dead. I loved my father's sense of humour. One time I was with my father in a store. I noticed that there was a guy with a broken arm. I asked my dad if he knew how that guy had broken his arm. My father replied, "He broke it raking leaves when he fell out of the tree."

In the morning we got up and made our way to a restaurant to get something to eat. We spent most of the day walking around and smoking cigarettes. That night we were going to one of the arcades that I frequented when my brother spotted me. My brother was two and a half years older than I was and considerably bigger than me. He made us both go home with him and stay in his room for the night. I wanted to run away really badly, but he stayed awake all night to make sure that I did not escape. The second that I tried to move he would sit up and look at me with an angry face. He wanted me to get caught by our mom.

In the morning he got up and brought my mother into the room, and when she saw me she was stunned. "Well, what are you doing here?" she asked me with surprise as my brother walked away. Then she ordered us to come sit in the kitchen while she made a phone call to the police to let them know where we were.

Man alive, Mom, I thought. *Aren't you even concerned about how I'm doing before you call the police? Do you care if I'm hungry or hurt?* I just shook my head in disbelief at my mom as I watched her call the police.

I leaned over and whispered to Scott that we had to run now or we would get caught. We jumped up and bolted out the door, running for about two blocks before stopping. We kept a low profile all day, hiding in back alleys and trying not to do anything that would get us into trouble.

Late in the afternoon we stole a cheque out of a car and then went to a restaurant to get something to eat. After we finished eating I wrote out the phoney cheque and then approached the waitress at the cash register to pay for the meal.

"I'm sorry, but we don't accept cheques here," she apologized.

"Well, my parents are just over there in that camper," I lied confidently. "I could go get some money and be right back."

"All right; I'll be here," she replied.

Scott and I walked out of the restaurant, and as soon as we reached the camper we had pointed to we went behind it and then ran. We went to the bus depot to try to stow away on a bus. However, we had to wait for a bus to come in. While waiting I decided to play a video game. I put a quarter into the machine, and it came right back out again. I tried it again, and it did the exact same thing again. It kept returning my coin, and I finally got really upset. I turned to Scott and told him I wanted to leave. Scott looked at me with bewilderment, wondering why I was so upset. I walked out of the bus depot, pushing the glass door open as hard as I could. To my surprise there was no door stopper and the door flew open, hit the brick building, and shattered with a loud smash. I took off and ran blindly down the street.

I came to a department store, went inside and walked around. I looked out the window to see if I could spot any police walking by who might be looking for me, but there were none to be found. I walked outside, lit up a cigarette, and tried to relax. I started to really think about what I was doing and what I was going to do next.

Should I turn myself in or go see my mother or keep running? I wondered. I weighed each option carefully. Actually, I was so confused that I did not know what to do next. I decided that

I had better go and see my mother. I walked to my house, about three miles away. I finally got to my house, ran inside, threw my arms around my mother, and started to cry.

"Are you okay, honey?" my mother asked as she looked at me with compassion. "Where did you go?" I didn't say anything.

My mother phoned the police and told them where I was. A little while later a cop showed up and took me down to the bus depot to ask me some questions. He showed me the glass door and asked me if I knew anything about it being broken. I lied and said I didn't know a thing about it. To my surprise I never heard another thing about it. There were many times when I should have been punished for things that I did wrong but never was.

Scott walked past the window at the bus depot, and the policeman saw him. The officer then motioned for him to come into the bus depot. A little while later a social worker picked us up and drove us back up to Lethbridge. Once again we were back at Sifton. We were then strip-searched, told to take showers, and sent to bed.

We were never physically punished for running away. However, we did lose certain privileges at the centre. For example, we were not allowed to go out to play in the backyard or play sports for a few days. We were not allowed to go on outings with the other kids. We couldn't watch television either. As our behaviour improved we would be given more and more privileges back.

I ran away one more time with Scott. We did not have any money, so we just walked around in Lethbridge looking for something to do. Scott ended up getting caught, and I took off. I managed to get away, but after some careful thought I decided to turn myself in. I walked into Sifton and waited for a staff worker to come over and talk with me. I glanced over to the dining room and noticed Scott sitting in his pyjamas at the table. It gave me an idea.

A staff worker approached me and said, "Come into the office. What made you decide to come back?"

"Well, there was nowhere else to go, and so I thought that rather than getting into more trouble I might as well come back," I replied, proud that I had told the truth for once.

"What are we going to do with you, Greg? You just keep running away. We're going to have to lock you up if you keep running," he stated.

"I'll make you a deal," I said as I remembered Scott in his pyjamas. "You give me back all of my privileges, but if I ever run away again you can put me in pyjamas for three days and take away all of my privileges."

He thought about it for a minute and then said, "Okay, that sounds like a fair deal to me. How about if I put it down in writing to make sure that we both keep our ends of the deal?"

So he wrote out a contract stating what I had agreed on, and we both signed it. I was a free man, with all of my privileges given back to me, and I had a clean slate.

The next day my social worker paid me a visit to talk with me about my behaviour. "I could have you sent to YDC in Edmonton and have you locked up for five months plus five months plus five months!" he threatened me, very annoyed.

"Well, I'm not going to run away any more," I told him angrily. I was upset that I was being threatened after setting things straight with the staff. I settled down after that, and I stayed at the centre for the summer. School was out, so it took pressure off me, and I was able to enjoy life at little more. I kept busy by playing sports at the centre with some of the other kids and going on day-long outings. Sometimes we would go to the store to get a treat.

I was allowed to phone my mother and father, so about once a week I would call my mom and talk to her. I would always ask her if I would be able to come back home and live there again, and she would reply that she was not ready for me to come home yet. I would always leave the conversation angry and hurt. I talked to my father less because he was not around home as much at night due to the fact that he was working.

Time went by, and the staff at the centre noticed that my behaviour had improved somewhat. My key worker asked me if I wanted to go home for a weekend to be with my mother. A key worker is a staff who is assigned to one child to take special note of his behaviour and progress.

"Sure, I would love to go home!" I agreed.

He made arrangements on a Friday to send me home for the weekend. A staff worker then drove me to the bus depot, bought me a ticket, and watched me board the bus. He stayed until the bus took off to make sure that I did not get off one bus and get onto another one. I arrived in Medicine Hat at about 6:30 that night and then I caught a bus to where my mother lived.

I visited my mother about three times during the course of the summer. When I came home for the visits we did not seem to spend time together, though. My mother never offered any suggestions for doing things with her. She did not know how to spend time with me, I guess. Instead I would go bike riding with my sister and play games with her. We would go to the park, or I would go buy a pack of cigarettes and we would go somewhere so that I could smoke where my mother wouldn't see me. Sometimes she would give me a couple of dollars so that I could go to the arcade and play games for a little while.

When it was time for me to leave I would say goodbye and catch a city bus down to the bus depot. I would board the bus for the trip back to Lethbridge, and as the bus pulled away I would start to cry. I just wanted things to be normal so that I could live at home with my mother.

I visited with my father a few times in the summer as well. He would pick me up with his truck at the bus depot, and we would go to his apartment. His girlfriend and her twin daughters were there too sometimes. They were really friendly, and I liked them. During these visits my father would talk to me and try to make sense of my problems. He would try to help me direct my behaviour so that I would not get into trouble any more. I just enjoyed being around him and having some time alone with him. He would barbecue, and we would talk while the food was cooking. Sometimes we would play cards and talk too. I am sure it hurt my father to see me having so much trouble with my life.

6 - A Change of Pace

The weeks rolled by, and late in July my key worker called me into the office. He said in a few weeks I would be moved to Medicine Hat to live with a man named Jerry Borgeau in a receiving home. I would be going on a camping trip with him that was to last for eight weeks.

I went to visit my mother one more time before going back to Sifton and then being sent to Jerry's. My visit was not good, though. We fought a lot, and I was upset about being moved to live with another person. I could not handle the instability of being moved around so much. I also stole some money from the house when I was there. My mother never found out about it until I was gone.

Saturday came, and it was time to go to the bus depot. As I walked downtown with my mother I thought about not being able to see her for two months. She left my side to go to the dentist's office for a few minutes to pay a bill while I continued on to the bus terminal. I started to get concerned because I wanted to say goodbye to her.

"So this is how it's going to end," I told myself painfully with tears in my eyes. "I have to go by myself, and she won't even say goodbye. Where is she? Why won't she come?" I wished that she had spent the last few minutes with me and then gone to the dentist's office.

A few minutes before the bus showed up she appeared. I gave her a hug and then grabbed my bags and got on the bus, sitting beside a window so I could see my mom. Slowly the bus started to move. I started to cry, waving to Mom. I continued to cry as we pulled away.

Mom stood there smiling, waving to me. *Can't you even cry, Mom? Don't you care about me?* I screamed silently. I cried half the way to Lethbridge as I smoked a few cigarettes.

The weeks rolled by at Sifton, and the day came when I was transferred to Jerry Borgeau's place. One of the staff members, Ian, drove me to the bus depot.

"Why don't you give me a smoke?" I asked politely.

"I can't, Greg," he said in a monotone voice. "If Social Services ever found out, I could lose my job. Why don't you come back when you're eighteen and I'll buy you a beer?"

"Yeah, I suppose," I replied, disappointed, wanting to drop the subject.

The trip home seemed long and boring. We stopped in Taber, and I bought a pack of cigarettes. When I arrived in Medicine Hat Jerry was waiting for me at the depot. He was about 5' 9" with light brown hair. His face was hard and stern. He seemed ready to defeat whatever stood in his way. I pulled my suitcase off the bus and shook his hand. We exchanged greetings and then walked toward his car. I put my suitcase in his trunk and we headed toward his place. I found out later that Jerry had served in the armed forces for some time. He also knew sign language very well and seemed to be quite intelligent.

When we arrived at his house I pulled the suitcase out of the trunk and started toward the front door while studying the outside of his house. It was finished with cedarwood. His yard was large and had lush bright green grass. There was a six foot fence surrounding his yard.

I was shown around the inside of the house and informed of my duties and chores. I met the other kids, four other guys from age fourteen to sixteen and one girl, who was ten. I also met Jerry's wife, Mary-Ann.

After supper we did some packing to get ready to leave the next day for an eight-week camping trip. His truck had a shell on the back so that we could put our gear in and ride in the back with it. We loaded our sleeping bags, suitcases, and tents into it.

The next morning we took off at 6:30 and headed toward the Rocky Mountains. We arrived at a campground at around three in the afternoon and set up our tents. Then the other guys and I played hide and seek in the trees. It was great being with other guys and having clean fun. I enjoyed the travelling and liked Jerry and the kids, but my sharp tongue worked against me.

By the end of the week everyone was angry with me, including Jerry. As we drove along the highway one of the older guys made tinfoil spitballs. Another guy held my mouth open while the first guy spit them into my mouth. I was gagging and crying, but they did not care and did not stop what they were doing. I think they were trying to teach me to keep my mouth shut by forcing me to keep it open. It worked, because I sure watched what I said after that.

We travelled through the Rocky Mountains from Alberta into British Columbia. We went through Lake Louise, Banff, saw Frank Slide, and even went hiking up a big mountain one day. It was beautiful scenery.

One day I was very homesick, and in tears I asked Mary-Ann if I could call my mom. She started to tease and ridicule me. "Oh, does the poor little baby miss his mom?" she taunted.

From that point on I hated her. "I wish you were dead," I said angrily but quiet enough so that she could not hear me. I was only twelve years old at the time. What did she expect?

One night I woke up in the middle of the night. I could not find the door to the tent, and I became claustrophobic. I started to yell and claw at the sides of the tent to try to get out. All of the guys started to wake up and panic. When they looked up from their sleeping bags all they could see was the shadow of something clawing at the tent, and they thought it was a bear. I guess unintentionally I was getting back at them for shooting spitballs into my mouth.

Our exploration of the country continued; however, everyone started to complain about having to sleep in tents and eat stew or beans every day. Jerry was getting tired of it. "If this keeps up we're going to go home," he threatened.

Good, I thought with hope, *then I won't have to sleep in this stupid tent any more.* I was sure negative at this point.

We kept on complaining, and Jerry could not take it any more. "That's it!" he finally said. "We're going home. Pack up and get into the truck." Angrily he continued to give orders until we were ready to leave. We piled into the back of the truck, and he drove for six straight hours, stopping only for gas.

When we arrived in Medicine Hat Jerry ordered us to unload the truck and put everything away. "You guys are going to do chores until the set date that we were supposed to arrive back in town."

We did chores for days and days after getting home. I was sick of yard work and of Jerry always ordering us around. I was ready to run away. If he pushed me once more I was going to take off.

He kept pushing and pushing, and finally I took off. As I ran down the street I remembered him saying that if we took off he would give us one hour to return and then he would phone the police. I spotted a truck just pulling out of a driveway. I ran over to it and banged on the window. A young woman rolled down the window.

"Can you guys drive me to Carswell Road?" I pleaded with desperation. "I need to get there right now."

"I'm sorry, but we're not going over there," the woman replied. I started to run again as fast as I could. I needed to get to my father's place before Jerry called the police.

A few seconds later the truck pulled up. "Jump in and we'll give you a ride," the woman offered. They drove me to my father's place and let me out. I thanked them over and over. Then I ran into the lobby of the apartment and rang my father's buzzer. He answered, and I told him it was me. He let me in, so I made my way to his apartment.

"What a surprise! I didn't expect to see you here," he said cheerfully.

I did not share his excitement. "Dad, I have a little problem. I ran away from where I was staying," I explained to him. "I don't know how to ask you this, Dad," I went on, with tears in my eyes, "but do you think I could come and live with you?"

"I don't think that would work out," he said regretfully.

We talked for a while, and then he phoned Jerry to explain my situation to him. Jerry came over a short while later to pick me up. "You can come over for a barbecue sometime, Greg," Dad said as we were getting ready to leave. Jerry drove me back to his house, and I spent the rest of the day doing chores.

The days were long and boring, and Jerry would not let me smoke. He let the older guys smoke, but not me. I was fed up with his policies and having to work all of the time. I ended up running away again, and I was picked up by the police. Jerry told the police that he did not want me there any more, so I was taken to YAC again. I stayed there for the night and then I was transferred back to Sifton in Lethbridge.

When I arrived at Sifton I recognized a lot of faces. Some of the staff workers even missed me a little. I settled down immediately. I did not want to push my luck and risk being sent somewhere else. I was running out of places to live.

My father was upset and wished I would have stayed in Medicine Hat so that he could visit me. He and my brother drove up one weekend to visit me. We went to a hotel and stayed there for a few nights. We went swimming and sat and visited throughout the day with each other. We even went to a pool hall and played pool together. I was sure glad to see them, and we had a great time together. It really made me miss my family, and I wished I had not taken them for granted.

I started school and was given grade eight work to do, even though I had not officially passed grade seven. But I applied myself and did okay. A new kid arrived, a Native Canadian named Darryl. He was two years older than me. We became close friends. I remember him coming up to me after he had been there about two days. "Hey, man," he whispered, "do you want to run away to Medicine Hat?"

I thought about it for a minute and then blurted out, "Sure, man. Why not? I've got nothing to lose."

The next day, Darryl and I and a couple of other kids were outside playing soccer with a staff worker. The staff worker went inside to get a Frisbee, and I immediately looked at Darryl.

"Let's go!" he whispered.

We jumped the fence and ran toward some houses to lose anybody who might try to chase us. We made our way downtown to a department store and stole some cigarettes. Then we left the store and stole a couple of bikes from a schoolyard. We started to ride toward Medicine Hat. We rode for about four hours and stopped in Taber. We went into a store, and Darryl stole some cookies, which we ate as we rode.

At around 10:30 that night we arrived in Burdett. It's about forty miles from Medicine Hat. I was very tired from riding a bike all day, so we decided to hide behind a bunch of trees and sleep until morning. Then we would get a fresh start the next day.

I laid down and was set to go to sleep. It was early in September, so it was quite warm out at night still.

"I'm going to go see if I can get a car," Darryl whispered.

"What do you mean, get a car?" I asked.

"I'm going to go see if I can get a car to steal," he replied.

"Fine," I said. "I'm going to see if I can get myself some sleep." I closed my eyes and started to relax.

A few minutes later Darryl returned and with excitement announced, "I found one! C'mon, man, let's go."

"Where is it?" I asked. My heart was pounding, and I felt really uneasy.

"Over there, in front of that hotel, the white truck," he calmly whispered.

"Okay. You start it up and pick me up on the highway," I told him nervously.

He nodded in agreement. I made my way over to the highway, walking backwards, watching in disbelief as he got into the truck and started it up. I shook my head and told myself that I was insane to do this. He pulled away from the hotel and picked me up. Then he turned left, and we drove toward Medicine Hat.

"This sure beats riding a bike, eh?" Darryl said joyfully.

"Yeah," I said, trying to share his excitement. But I was very nervous. I kept looking back to see if anyone was following us. I looked around in the truck and noticed that there was a rifle on a rack mounted above the window.

When we pulled into Medicine Hat, I noticed that there was a set of headlights that seemed to be following us. When we turned the corner the lights were very close to us. I caught a glimpse of the car behind us when we turned. I felt like my heart had jumped into my throat as it pounded hard. "It's an RCMP!" I shrieked. "What are we gonna do, man?"

"Calm down," Darryl replied, trying to keep me from panicking so bad.

The cruiser put on his flashing lights, signalling for us to pull over. *I knew I should've stayed sleeping under that tree,* I told myself as I sulked. *I knew it, I just knew it.*

We both sat impatiently in the truck as another RCMP cruiser pulled up. "Why would they send out two cruisers to get us?" Darryl wondered. "That's pretty weird. You'd think they'd just come and get us."

"Come out of the truck with your hands above your head," a voice ordered us through a megaphone.

Darryl and I stepped out of the truck with our hands in the air.

"Step away from the truck," the voice ordered us.

We obeyed, and then an officer cautiously walked toward us, shut the door of the truck, and told us to come with him. He brought us over to his cruiser, and we both got into the back. We were then taken to the RCMP station for questioning. As we drove toward the station Darryl asked, "Why did you wait for a second cruiser to come before doing anything?"

The officer replied, "Because there was a firearm present in the truck. We never do anything by ourselves when a gun is involved; we always wait for a backup unit. Besides, we didn't know it was just a couple of kids in the truck. It could have been wanted criminals for all we knew."

After some questioning we were taken to YAC, given something to eat, and sent to bed. *My dad is gonna kill me*, I thought with panic. *He is probably going to want to torture me for a while first though.* "Oh God," I prayed in desperation, "if You get me out of this I'll never steal again."

The next day Darryl and I received a summons to appear in court. I was restless every day until our court date rolled around.

A cop came up to YAC to escort us to the courthouse. "I don't shoot above the head; I shoot for the head," I remember him telling us as he attempted to discourage us from running away. We were driven to the courthouse in a police cruiser. I saw an orange truck parked outside on the street—my father's. *He's gonna kill me,* I said to myself, full of fear.

In the courtroom it was the same as before. When the judge asked me if I had stolen the truck, I innocently replied, "Does that mean stealing the truck or does it mean getting in and going for a ride?"

"If you wish to discuss the matter with Greg, you can," the judge suggested to my father. My father motioned for me to step out of the door with him, and I followed.

"You know if you stole the truck or not," he said quietly. "I don't think that there is any question in your mind; you know what you did."

We made our way back into the courtroom.

"Did you, Gregory Todd Van Riper, steal this truck?" the judge asked me quietly.

"Yes, I did," I replied.

The only thing I can remember happening after that was watching my social worker stand up and politely ask if I could be placed into a home somewhere in Medicine Hat. The judge remarkably complied, and I was placed in a receiving home in Medicine Hat for a six-month period.

Darryl and I were taken back to YAC in a cage in the back of a van. "What did you get?" I asked Darryl.

"Uh, I gotta wait around until next week for my next court day," he said, depressed. "What did you get?"

"I get to stay in Medicine Hat for a while."

I was kept at YAC until my clothes arrived from Sifton. Darryl had his court case postponed for another week, and I never saw him again.

In the afternoon my clothes arrived; then I was picked up by my social worker and taken to my new home. It was a large house with a wood finish. It had a large circular driveway and a large yard. I was let into the house and met my new guardians. "This is Marilyn and her husband, Marcel," my social worker introduced me.

"Hi," I said timidly.

"Hi" the woman replied coldly. "Put your stuff downstairs in the room on the left."

My worker talked with us for a while and then said goodbye to me. I turned and looked at Marilyn. "Can I wash my hair?" I asked.

"Yup. The bathroom is down the hall from your room and on the right," she replied.

I washed my hair, then lit up a cigarette and watched television for a while. Marilyn had two boys and one girl of her own. She also had two other foster kids there, both girls.

That night I was walking down the steps to go to my room when I stopped and overheard her talking with one of her sons. "Is this guy a troublemaker, or did he come from a broken home?" her son asked.

"He's a troublemaker," Marilyn replied.

"What did he do?"

"He stole a truck."

"He stole a truck? He's that bad? How do you expect to keep him here?" her son exclaimed in disbelief.

"I don't," she answered bluntly.

They don't even want me here. Then why did she let me come here to live? I thought with frustration. I was already in Marilyn's bad books even though I had not done anything yet to offend her.

The next day when I woke up I went to school and met up with a few people I had known before I was sent away. They were friendly toward me even though they knew some of the things about my past. *They must have forgotten the past,* I thought.

I attended school and did grade eight work for three weeks. I started to get bored with school and began to skip out. The principal found out and called my foster mother. I ended up getting kicked out of school for three days. Marilyn came and picked me up from school. Was she ever upset with me too! She chewed me out all the way home. "I'm so disgusted with you that I don't even want to talk to you," I remember her complaining to me.

I did not care though; she always seemed to be upset with me. I sure was off to a great start at my new home.

There was no point in only having a few people angry with me. I might as well have everyone mad at me. That was how I lived and behaved, trying to make everyone mad at me, even though I did not do it intentionally. It was partly to do with my attachment disorder.

During the three days that I was out of school Marilyn made me stay home and clean her house. I washed all of the walls, I scrubbed the bathrooms, and I vacuumed the whole house. I washed her car, too. It was not hard work, but it kept me busy.

The school principal phoned Marilyn and notified her that I was to transfer to another school. The teachers at that school had had enough of me. I made friends at my new school very quickly. Then I went back to my old boss and asked him if I could have my old job back.

"As long as you have your head screwed on straight you can have your job back," he said, slowly and carefully.

One day when I was sweeping out garbage stalls I got an idea to steal some blank cheques and forge them to get some extra money. I went over to my boss's truck and grabbed some blank cheques before he came back. I carefully folded them and put them into my pocket. After I finished my job I went to his office and asked him to write me out my cheque for working. He wrote out my usual ten dollar cheque, and I took off.

I copied his signature from my paycheque onto all of the stolen cheques by holding them up against a window. They were perfect—except for one thing. My boss had made a mistake on my paycheque, and I copied the mistake onto all of the others. I cashed all of them at the grocery store close to where I lived, where everyone knew me. Then I went to visit my mother, because it was Thanksgiving weekend.

Later on that night while I was down at the arcade spending all of my money, one of the store clerks came down to the arcade and started to talk to me. "C'mere! I want to show you something," he said.

I followed him to the store, not even thinking that I was in any kind of trouble. He showed me the mistakes on the cheques. "See this?" he said with a concerned look. "Mistake, mistake, mistake."

Fear started to well up inside of me and my heart started to pound rapidly. "What are you going to do?" I asked, starting to panic.

"Well, we could send them through to the bank, but they would find the mistakes for sure. We could call your boss and see what he wants to do. You know, just get it over with tonight. Because when the bank finds out they'll phone your boss anyway. So what do you want to do?" he asked impatiently.

"What if I give you back the money and you tear up the cheques?" I asked, hoping he would have mercy on me.

"I can't do that. What you did was dishonest, and we have to deal with it," he told me firmly while tapping the cheques with his finger.

"Then phone my boss," I said angrily, having lost all hope of getting off the hook.

Hot tears of anger started to form in my eyes as he picked up the phone. "You can wait in the back of the store if you want," he told me.

I walked to the back of the store and went through a set of swinging doors that had two small windows in them. I peered through to see what was happening. I watched my boss enter the store, followed by the police. I saw the look on my boss's face as he picked up the cheques and shook his head in disbelief. I remembered at that point how I had told him that my head was screwed on straight.

I turned around and looked down at the floor. I knew that I would be going back to YAC, so I started to look for a way to escape. There was a set of double doors in front of me where the big food trucks unloaded. The doors were locked, and a big steel padlock held them shut. If I could get that lock off I might be able to get out of there. But a minute later it did not matter anyway. The policeman came through the back and told me to come with him.

"Where to?" I asked.

"To YAC," he replied.

The officer drove me my mother's house and told her what had happened. She looked at me with concern and asked, very frustrated, "Why did you do it?"

"I don't know!" I yelled to her angrily.

I was then escorted to YAC by the police. It was Thanksgiving weekend, and I was sitting in YAC, miserable and frustrated. I had nobody to blame but myself though.

I was given a room and started to put my clothes away. "Oh Lord," I said with tears in my eyes, "if You get me out of here, I'll never steal again."

I had to wait until Tuesday to go to court, since Monday was a holiday. My mother came and brought me a piece of pumpkin pie. She stayed and talked with me for a while, trying to make me feel better. She had to take the bus all the way to YAC, which was probably an hour trip to get across the city and then another hour to get back home.

On Tuesday I was escorted to the courthouse by the police. I do not remember anything about that court appearance except that my father was not present. I was told to go to school after court.

After school I was riding home on the bus, and one of the kids from my foster home looked over at me with surprise. "Aren't you supposed to be in Edmonton Youth Detention Centre?" she asked with concern.

I shook my head nonchalantly and replied, "I never heard anything about it."

I arrived at my foster home, walked into the house, and Marilyn started to threaten me. "You'd better shape up and stay out of trouble, because I've had it with you!" she screamed.

The next couple of days I tried very hard to stay out of trouble. I just went to school and behaved.

I went to my father's on Sunday and rang the buzzer to his apartment. He answered the door and let me in. I went upstairs hoping to have a good visit with him. This was the first time that I had had any contact with him since getting into trouble with the law again. I did not realize that I would not stay very long.

I sat down on the couch, and my father started to talk to me. He was very disappointed about what I had done. He told me that he did not think it was going to work with me coming over and being around him at this point. "Greg, I just don't think it is good for us to be around each other right now," he said, trying to be calm. He walked me to the door of his apartment and opened it for me to leave.

I was very hurt and left the apartment angry. I did not try to contact him again after that. I felt very detached from my parents at this point in my life. I had been abandoned and rejected so much, due to my behaviour but also from my father drinking so much and my mother not being there for me emotionally.

7 - Home on the Range

On Halloween night I went out trick or treating with a friend from school. Although I knew I should have gone back to Marilyn's, I ended up staying overnight at his house. I thought she might show some leniency because I had been good for a couple of weeks.

When I returned the next day, Marilyn freaked out on me. As she started to scream at me I lit up a smoke and just stood there listening to her yell at me. I ate supper and headed to bed early that night.

As I walked past her daughter's bedroom something got my attention. It was a UNICEF (United Nations Children's Fund) box, filled with Halloween donations. I jumped into the room and grabbed the box. Then I went downstairs to bed. I hoped that it would not be missed that night or I wouldn't be the first suspect to be blamed for it.

The next day I went to school with the box in my coat pocket. I went to my locker and emptied the change out into my pockets. I sorted the silver from the pennies. Then I spent some of the money on cigarettes and food. I wasn't even worried about getting caught.

At about 2:30 in the afternoon I was sitting in French class writing, and there was a knock at the door. "Greg, there's someone here to see you," my teacher informed me.

I got up from my desk, looked out the door, and saw a man about 5'10" with a beard. He was dressed in a suit and was holding a briefcase. "Come with me," he politely ordered.

"Where are we going?"

"Just down to the office," he said quietly. "You're getting transferred to another foster home."

"Where's the home?" I asked.

"Out on a farm."

"A farm!" I said with disgust.

We walked together into the office and I waited for him to talk with the principal. *I hate farms, I hate animals, and most of all I hate being away from the city!* I thought angrily.

The bearded man walked out of the office and told me to go upstairs to get my books. Angry and bitter, I stormed upstairs and walked into my classroom.

"And where do you think you're going?" my teacher asked.

"To hell!" I screamed angrily. Little did I know that hell on earth was exactly where I was going.

I made my way back down the stairs to the office and placed my books onto the counter. Then I walked out of the office and got into a car with the man, whom I later learned was my new social worker. He drove me to my old foster home, and we picked up my clothes.

"Why am I being moved?" I asked.

"All I know is that your present foster parents want you out of that house now," he told me, his voice sharing their disgust.

I put my suitcase in the car, and he drove toward the south part of town, right past all of the houses and onto a dirt road. I was surrounded by prairie now, and I hated it. He continued to drive until we were about five miles south of town. He turned left at a white house, which was hidden behind a bunch of trees. There were barns and sheds all over the yard.

As we pulled into the yard I lit up a cigarette. I stepped out of the car, and a guy was waiting at the side of the house for me. His name was Jerry. He was about 6' tall and weighed about 190 pounds. He had long blond curly hair and was wearing dirty farm clothes.

"You better put that out," he said, in a way that implied that if I did not, some supernatural being might get me. "C'mon in," he offered with a friendly voice.

I put out my cigarette and walked into the house. A woman turned and greeted me. "Hi, how are you doing?" she asked with a friendly voice. She turned around and tended to her cooking once again. She was about 5'1" and had dark black hair. She was kind of plump and had a friendly sort of face. She looked like she was about forty-five years old. Her name was Alice.

"Good," I replied with hesitation.

"Let's go do the chores," Jerry said. "You can wear those clothes."

I followed him across a small bridge that was built over an irrigation ditch, and we stopped when we got to a haystack.

"Grab a bale of hay," Jerry ordered.

I grabbed a bale. I only weighed about ninety pounds, and I could not lift it. So I ended up rolling it on the ground to the barn where the cows were being milked. "How many of these do we have to move?" I whined.

"Oh, about five or six," he replied.

Already I hated this place and wanted to leave. I looked toward the house and saw my social worker getting into his car to leave. I wanted to go and talk to him. I wanted to run to his car and tell him that I wanted to go somewhere else. But there was probably nowhere else for me to go.

I entered the cow barn and watched three people milking cows. The milking parlour held six cows at a time, and there were ten cows to milk. My next job was to break off a chunk of hay and give it to the cows while they were being milked.

After all of the cows were milked and taken out of the barn, I had to shovel all of the manure from the barn into the barnyard. When I finished, Jerry ordered me to go up to the house with him.

"Do you think I would be able to wash my hair tonight?" I asked Jerry politely.

"It's a privilege, and you have to earn it," he replied.

"What do you mean, I have to earn it?" I asked with frustration.

"It's a privilege, and you have to work to earn it," he replied aggressively.

We walked into the house, and I was given some clean clothes to wear around the house. I walked into the bathroom and was told to wash my socks in the toilet. They were dirty from doing chores. After I finished washing my socks I asked Jerry if he wanted me to flush the toilet. He replied no, but out of habit I flushed it anyway. Jerry slapped me on the back of my head very firmly. Then he pointed at me with his index finger and said forcefully, "When I tell you to do something, you better listen."

"I'm sorry, okay?" I begged, wanting to make everything all right.

"Yeah," he replied with no emotion.

We sat down to eat supper and had hot dogs and potato salad. I met the rest of the kids at the table before we started to eat. There were six younger kids (two were girls) and five older kids. The older kids were all very big and well built. They were allowed to discipline us if they thought that we were being bad. This included slapping our faces as hard as they wanted, hitting us with a closed fist, or even making us do up to 1,000 push-ups.

Alice had all of the kids line up and give her their plates while she dished out our food. She really heaped the food onto my plate. I was not used to eating that much, but I was forced to eat it all anyway.

As I was eating I accidentally hit my teeth with my fork.

"Don't hit your teeth with your fork," Alice warned me.

I looked at her with bewilderment. *What difference does it make if I hit my teeth or not?*

"Answer her," Jerry commanded.

"Huh?"

"When somebody says something to you, I want you to answer them," he explained to me with aggression in his voice again.

"All right," I replied, perplexed.

I started eating some more, and a few minutes later I accidentally hit my teeth with my fork again. Jerry reached over and grabbed a good handful of my hair. Then he tilted my head and slapped me on the face very hard about three times. "Don't hit your teeth with your fork," he snapped at me. "You have to apologize."

"I'm sorry for hitting my teeth with my fork," I confessed to Alice as tears started to well up in my eyes. She looked at me like I had held her up and taken her money. It was like I had personally assaulted her.

Her husband, Wilf, was sitting next to her. He was about 5'8" with light brown greying hair. He was a friendly sort of fellow and never raised his voice to me in the two years that I was in this home. Alice was the one who seemed to wear the pants in the marriage.

After supper we did the dishes. Jerry handed me a towel and told me to dry the dishes. A few seconds later Mason, one of the other younger foster kids, accidentally banged one plate against another while putting it down.

"Don't do that again," threatened Jerry.

"Okay. I'm sorry," Mason replied very meekly.

A few minutes passed, and Mason banged another plate by accident. Jerry put down his dish towel, grabbed a handful of Mason's hair, and slapped him eight times on the face, very hard. I gasped in disbelief. Jerry noticed my reaction and then grabbed my hair, tilted my head, and slapped me three times on my face. "You don't feel sorry for someone when they are getting disciplined!" he said with an angry voice. "I didn't hear you answer either," he growled.

"Okay," I replied with a weak voice while wiping tears from my eyes.

All night long I saw kids getting hit for the most petty things. *What kind of a place is this?* I thought with horror.

After the dishes were finished all of the kids went and did their homework. "Could I please have my coat?" I asked Jerry very humbly.

"What for?" he snapped.

"I just want to get some fresh air," I lied. Actually, I wanted to run away.

Sitting right beside Jerry was a guy named Dwight. He was six feet tall and about 180 pounds of solid muscle. He had a broken leg, too.

"If you're thinking of running away you can forget about it," Jerry warned me, almost reading my mind. "You see his leg? He tried running away last month, and I caught him and broke his leg."

I later learned that Dwight had broken his leg while jumping down a flight of stairs. But from the things I had seen to that point I believed Jerry.

"Can I go to the bathroom?" I asked Jerry later on.

"Yeah. Put your shoes on," he replied.

I put my shoes on, and then we went outside to an outhouse located twenty yards from the house. "This is where you go to the bathroom," Jerry informed me. "The only time you can use the bathroom in the house is after we are in the house for the night."

For the next two years, during summer and winter, I used the outhouse. It was not bad in the summer. In the winter, though, it was very uncomfortable sitting on an ice-cold seat. The old-timers must have been tough.

Alice told me to read my Bible before I went to bed. I read part of it and then was shown where to sleep. I slept in a room with four other people. There were four of us on two sets of bunk beds, and Mike (one of the older guys) slept on the floor in front of the door so that nobody would try to get out of the room to run away.

At 5:45 the next morning an alarm clock went off. Jerry ordered me to get up along with the other guys because it was chore time. We then went over to the entryway to get our chore clothes on. All of the guys were assigned certain chores. The girls stayed in bed until 6:30, and then they had to walk back and forth about a 50 metre distance until breakfast was ready. They had two separate paths to walk on. They did this for eight or nine hours a day sometimes. There were deep paths carved out where they had walked for those many hours.

I went with Jerry to the cow barn and fed the cows some hay while they were being milked.

"My cow needs some hay," Miles ordered me.

"Okay," I answered.

I threw some hay to the cow, and the cow got spooked. "You scared my cow," Miles said with disgust. "C'mere."

I walked over to Miles, and he drilled me across the face with his hand. "Don't do it again!" he barked. Miles was about 5'10" and 160 pounds. He handed out the most discipline and loved to cause trouble so that he could hit the kids.

When we were finished milking the cows I went with Miles up to the house and got changed into some school clothes. We had three sets of clothes to wear at the foster home. One set was for doing chores. One set was for around the house, and the other set was for school.

"Everyone come to the table," Alice called.

All of the kids came out to the kitchen and sat down at the table. Alice came down the stairs and sat down. She meticulously inspected all of the kids. Then she opened up a big green Bible and started to read. When she finished reading she prayed, and then we all grabbed some toast to eat very quickly. We then did the dishes and ran out the door to catch the bus at the edge of the yard.

Jerry made me sit with him at the back of the bus. As the bus pulled out of the yard Jerry turned and threatened me, "If you run away today I'm going to break your legs." But his warning did not sway my will at all. I was determined to get out of this place.

We were taken to a school in Irvine, a little farm town about twenty miles east of Medicine Hat on the TransCanada Highway. As we drove on the bus toward Irvine I put my head against the window of the bus and thought about my own home. *Why won't you phone me, Mom?* I thought as tears welled up in my eyes.

We pulled into the parking lot and the bus door opened. The school had grades one to twelve in it. There were about 350 students at this school, most of them country kids. Jerry escorted me to my class. A bunch of unfamiliar faces stared at me with curiosity. Most of the guys were wearing belts with big buckles and cowboy boots. *I'm sure going to get along with these guys,* I thought. *Everyone is so friendly.*

My classroom was filled with country kids. As I look back now I can recall many times listening to them making very humorous remarks about different situations. They were very intelligent and funny people, but at that point I did not know how to relate to them. If I had, my life at school would have been markedly different, with many more positive experiences and relationships.

The announcements came on, and we sang "O Canada." The teacher gave me some textbooks, and we were given an assignment.

At lunchtime I went to my locker to get my lunch and put my books away. I started to walk toward the door that led outside so that I could eat my lunch. I looked up, and there were three foster kids standing at the door. "Don't even think of running away," Miles hissed at me.

Actually, I was not planning to run away. I was only going to go outside to eat my lunch. At my school in Medicine Hat we were not allowed to stay in the classrooms to eat. I also knew better than to run away when a whole bunch of people were around.

We went to shop class after lunch, and one of the kids took my pencil away from me. I put him in a headlock and squeezed his head so hard that he could not breathe by the time I let go. He gave back my pencil, and I did not say a word to anyone else.

By the next class I decided that I had had enough. The teacher gave me permission to go to the bathroom. I went to my locker and quietly got my jacket. Then I took off out the door.

My heart was beating very fast as I started to run toward the highway. I was trying to think of how to get to Medicine Hat without getting caught. I spotted a bike behind a beat-up old house. I ran over, grabbed the bike, and started to pedal toward town.

I have to ride as fast as I can go, I told myself frantically. *If Jerry catches me, he'll break both of my legs.*

As I think about this now I am reminded of the kid who told his mother to watch him as he rode his bike with no hands. His mother said, "If you fall off of your bike and break both of your legs, don't come running to me."

I rode about two miles and spotted a house. I rode up to it and rang the doorbell. "Hi," I said trying to sound friendly. "You're not going to Medicine Hat, are you?"

"No. I'm sorry, but we didn't make any plans to go into town today," the woman replied apologetically. I could see that this woman did not want anything to do with me because I looked very suspicious. I jumped back on my stolen bike and started to ride. But I was more fearful and desperate now.

The next house was about a quarter mile away. I rode up to the door and asked the same question. I did not know that Alice had a relative whose house I was now at. I don't remember what she said, but her statement indicated that she knew who I was and who I was running from. What are the odds that I would end up at the house of a relative of Alice's? I should have bought a lottery ticket.

I jumped back onto my bike, and out of the corner of my eye I saw a school bus stopping. The house I was at was only a short distance from the main highway. Two kids got off the bus. Jerry must have seen me because he got off the bus too and started running toward the house.

It's Jerry! I panicked. *He's gonna punch me out.* My heart started to pound as I pedalled away from the house. By the time Jerry arrived at the house, Alice's relative had started up her truck, and she drove toward him and picked him up.

I looked back and saw them coming. I stopped my bike, knowing that I was going to get caught. The truck pulled up, Jerry jumped out and put my bike into the back of the truck, and we drove down to the house. We walked into the house and Jerry made a phone call. I sat in a chair and was very fearful, because I did not know what was going to happen to me.

Fifteen minutes later I saw Alice driving toward the house in her van. Jerry ordered me to go outside. As the van pulled up to the house Jerry grabbed my coat and pushed me onto the ground very hard, and my hands got all scraped up. He opened the door to the van and told me to get in and sit on the floor. Then Alice turned to me and with a closed fist punched me in the face about eight times, very hard. "How can you run from people who are trying to help you?" she yelled. "It's ordained by God for you to be here with us!"

"I was going to push him in front of the van, but I thought I better not," Jerry said to Alice.

As we drove back to the farm, I licked my lips to see if there was any blood on them. I wished I had gotten away so I wouldn't have to put up with her and Jerry. Then I wouldn't get beat up any more.

When I arrived at the farm all of the kids started calling me names and making fun of me as they walked past me while doing their chores. Then Jerry looked at me and said with a sarcastic voice, "If you think running is so great, then run." I was forced to run from the chicken barn to the garage, about 70 metres.

I ran back and forth for about forty-five minutes while Dwight supervised me. Every time I started to slow down he would prod me with his crutch. "Get running!" he would yell angrily. Sometimes he would hit me with his crutch as I ran past him. "Are you still going to run away?" he would taunt. If a foster kid happened to be going in the same direction as I was running, he would push me and call me names.

After what seemed like forever I was told to go into the house and wash up for supper. Then I sat at the kitchen table and looked up at Alice with fear in my eyes.

"I don't like your attitude," she said with disgust. Then she slid her chair back, got up, grabbed me by the hair, and slapped my face about five times. I didn't know how she could determine what my attitude was, because she did not know what I was thinking.

"I didn't hear you answer," she shrieked at me. Then she belted me a couple more times.

"Okay," I said, as tears welled up in my eyes.

She watched me like a hawk as I ate supper. "Hold your fork with the same hand that you pick up your milk with," she ordered me. "Don't pick up your milk in one hand and have a forkful of food in the other," she barked. "Don't hit your teeth with your fork, and sit up straight," she bellowed.

"Jerry do you want to look after this? He just hit teeth with his fork again," she complained.

Jerry got up, grabbed me by the hair, and slapped me about seven times. "Quit being ornery!" he yelled.

I sat back down and ate my supper very carefully, trying

to coddle my battered face. *What difference does it make how I hold my fork?* I thought, bewildered.

I managed to get through supper without getting hit again and then did the dishes. As I dried a plate it accidentally hit another one. Alice asked Dwight to take care of it. Dwight took me out into the entryway and told me to put my hands by my side. Then he leaned back, and as he moved forward he punched me square in the stomach. The wind was knocked clear out of me. Tears welled up in my eyes as I went back to drying the dishes.

Someone had dropped by my class and gotten my homework, so I did that next. Then I was told to read my Bible and go to bed.

No matter where I went or what I did, I had to ask for permission. After I was given permission, Jerry or one of the other older kids would follow me. They were much older than me and a lot bigger. They assisted Alice in disciplining the six younger kids. Every time I did something that I was not supposed to do, I was hit. I was told how to and when to eat, drink, sleep, get dressed, and work. I was told how to look and feel, when to be happy and when to be sad or angry. If Alice saw me doing something and did not like the way I was doing it, she would yell at me, slap me, and command it to be done the way she wanted it done.

This foster home was different from all of the other ones I had been at before. Normally the kids were united against the guardians to some extent, or it was every man for himself and nobody really cared what anybody else did. Most of the time the kids would not co-operate with the foster parents or guardians; they would rebel. But this place was different. The kids were always telling on each other to try and get other kids in trouble so that they themselves would not get beaten. The only way to avoid being beaten up was to tell on someone else. Everyone watched everyone else like a hawk, and as soon as a mistake was made they would go and tell Alice. She would then start giving out discipline. It was not like in Sifton when a kid would ask another kid to run away with him. I could not trust anyone or tell anybody anything.

I would also earn the approval of Alice if I told on someone else. I told on some of the kids to get the attention off of me so that I would not be beaten. Then Alice would say, "Thank you, Greg, for being so responsible and letting me know how foolish Mason was acting." None of the kids would ever confront me about telling on them, because I would just go to Alice and tell her what happened. She would then give that person a beating.

When Alice found out about one of the kids doing something wrong she would confront him or her at the table in front of everyone else so that the rest of the kids would hear it. She would encourage and welcome all of the other kids to join her in ridiculing and mocking the kid who was at fault. She strategically orchestrated her tactics perfectly while pitting everyone against each other so that there would be no alliances formed between the kids. It was everyone against each other.

8 - Whipped into Shape

I resented the fact that I had to call Alice "Mom." When I woke up in the morning I had to say, "Good morning, Mom." Before I went out the door to go to school I had to say, "Bye, Mom. I love you." If I did not call her Mom and say "I love you" I would get hit and ridiculed by the other kids or cross-examined by Alice. It would cause a lot of extra conflict, and sometimes beatings would follow. So I did it, to avoid being hit and teased.

Alice was very critical of everything that I did. When she read the Bible each morning she would ask a few of us kids to pray. I would pray sometimes, and if she did not like what I was saying she would interrupt and tell me what to say.

One time we were at a wedding of a close friend of hers, and the bride was saying her vows. At she continued to speak she was overcome with emotion and started to cry. Alice perceived it as the bride putting on a show of crying to get extra attention. How much more attention could the bride in a wedding get?

Many times the social workers would phone out to the farm and announce to Alice that they were coming out to visit. Alice would call all of us inside and tell us to get our good clothes on. Then she would tell the older kids to get banana bread out, cut it up, and to make coffee. "If you turn on the tears when that social worker comes out here, you'll get it when she leaves," Alice would threaten us all.

The social worker would come out, and we would sit in the kitchen until we were called. One by one we would file through the living room, shake her hand, and smile like programmed robots. Not once did a social worker ever talk to me alone to find out how things were going or if my needs were being met. They never questioned if we were being taken care of properly or if everything was all right.

I recall one time overhearing Mason talking with his social worker. The worker asked him if he wanted to go and live with his mom, and he replied, "Yes, that's where I really want to be!"

Alice was sitting right there, and after the worker left he got into a lot of trouble for saying what was in his heart. Alice bugged him about it in front of all the kids. "That's really where I want to be," she would mimic, mocking him. "You just want to go home, but you're just going to return to your old way of life again. It doesn't matter where you are; you'll be discontent and slip back into your old ways again. You're always wishing you were somewhere else. You're never satisfied with what you have. 'Poor me, I'm so hard done by,' and you can justify yourself all the way to hell and talk until you're blue in the face, but it won't do any good," she would say over and over every day. I think that she was insulted that he didn't want to stay and live with her at the foster home.

Alice often spoke about how cruel her brothers had been to her when she was growing up. She would tell us stories about when she would be cleaning the house or working and her brothers would be hurting her or mistreating her in some way. Then she would say, “And I didn’t know if there was a God, but if there was I wished He would have struck me dead.”

Another thing she would do is threaten us that God would strike us dead if we did something wrong. For example, if Alice found out that one of the kids had cheated on a test she would say, “You’re lucky that the good Lord didn’t strike you dead when you did that,” with a very condemning voice. I was so used to her hitting me when I did something wrong that I started to believe what she said about God doing the same thing. She would also tell us about young people dying of heart trouble or getting killed instantly and said it could happen to us as well. She would say, “You never know when you might be driving down the road, get in an accident, be killed, and end up in a lost eternity in hell. So you’d better be right with God.“

She told us about a seventeen-year-old who had died of a heart attack. “The day before yesterday he was walking down the street and he just fell over dead,” she told us, with a message of warning in her voice. “You’d better be right with God, because you never know when your time will come.

In the two years that I was there she told us lots of stories like this one. She so often repeated phrases about God wanting to kill me or get me that I started to believe her after a while. Her words influenced me tremendously. I started to have trouble sleeping at night because I was fearful that God might strike me dead or hurt me. I started to have panic attacks at home too.

At night the panic attacks seemed worse. I would lie in bed and wonder if this would be the night when God would kill me. I wondered if I had been good enough to stay alive one more day or not. I could not tell anyone how I felt, because they would laugh at me. I would lie in bed and cry as I pleaded, "Please don't kill me, God! I'll try to be better." This would go on for half the night until I finally fell asleep from exhaustion.

I was constantly on guard to make sure that I did not do something worthy of a beating either. It was very stressful seeing others being beaten every day and being beaten myself. The fear got worse and worse as time went on. Sometimes I would be sitting at the table and start to have a panic attack. I remember one time at the table this happened while Alice was praying. So I started to make a noise, because I thought that if I made a noise while I was starting to die that someone might be able to save me. Alice stopped praying and looked up at me. She had no idea what was going through my mind at that point. "That pain you have in your stomach is nothing compared to the pain you're going to feel in hell if you keep that up," she warned me angrily.

I started to believe that God was a lot like Alice, because of what she said and did. She would say things like "God told me what you did when you cheated on that test." It was like she thought she had an open line with God and that everyone else did not. Sometimes she was right about certain things. But sometimes she was wrong.

Some of us would confess that we did something wrong even if it we didn't do it, so that we wouldn't get a worse beating. Then Alice would say, "God told me that you broke that lamp." As long as I was behaving perfectly I would not be punished. But as soon as I did something wrong I would be beaten or disciplined. I thought that

God was finally going to get me for being so bad. I thought for sure that God was going to kill me at any moment. I went through this over and over every day at the foster home.

At breakfast time every morning after we were all gathered at the table Alice would open her big green Bible and read to us. Sometimes she would read 1 Corinthians 13. It says that love is patient, kind, not easily angered or irritable. The list goes on with a beautiful description of love. After she finished reading it, sometimes she would look at one of the kids and get upset because she thought he or she was giving her a mean look. She would become agitated and beat the kid severely. I never understood how she could read about love to us from the Bible and not set an example. She did the exact opposite of what the Bible said. Her words and actions gave a conflicting message. She always told us that God was a God of love, but she was more concerned about catching us when we were doing something wrong.

Calvin Miller wrote:

> Malicious truth gloats like a conqueror. Loving truth mourns that it must confront and show a brother his error. Malicious truth struts at its power. Loving truth weeps to find that the correction it inspires may for a while cause great pain. Malicious truth cries, "Checkmate, you are beaten!" Loving truth whispers, "I correct you with the same pain you feel. But when the pain is over, we shall rejoice that honesty and love have been served" (Calvin Miller, "To Be Perfectly Honest," *Moody Monthly*, March 1987).

Alice cried "Checkmate" with us kids constantly. Her favourite motto for running the home was "spare the rod, spoil the child," based on her favourite verse, Proverbs 13:24. Many times she would beat us or have one of the older kids beat us and we would wind up with bruises or fat lips. She would then accuse us of inflicting ourselves with the injury because we rubbed our eyes or bit our lips. She could not accept the fact that our injuries were caused by being beaten. If I woke up in the morning and rubbed my eyes, Alice would accuse me of trying to give myself a black eye. I would be sitting at the table and she would say, "Look at Greg, trying to give himself a black eye. He's sure working on that eye."

Push-ups were another form of punishment at this home. If something in the house got broken, Alice would make the kids she thought were involved line up on the floor on their hands and knees while facing the wall. Sometimes the one who broke the object was not even among those lined up. She would make them stay there until one of them confessed. If nobody confessed she would pick the one she thought was guilty and make him or her do 1,000 push-ups. Some days we were forced to do up to 2,000 push-ups. When a person's body gave out from physical exhaustion, Alice would take a long black rubber hose and hit him with it on his backside to try to make him do more. Lots of times I was beaten and forced to confess to things I had never done.

We were not allowed to take food from the fridge without asking Alice or Wilf. If we took food without permission, Alice referred to it as stealing. If we were caught, Alice would beat us or hit us with the black rubber hose. One night Mason got up and went into the fridge. It must have been about two or three in the morning. I was woken up by the sound of Mason screaming as Alice hit him with the rubber hose again and again. The next morning when we went into the entryway of the house to get changed into our chore clothes, I saw that Mason's legs were all black and blue. They were cut and very red. It looked very painful. He moved very slowly as he got changed. I knew what he was going through because I had gone through it too.

If I did something wrong that was deserving of the rubber hose, Alice or Wilf would make me pull my pants and underwear down and then bend over. I would have to stay that way, motionless, as I was hit on my backside.

Every Sunday we would all go to church. Lots of times it was very hard to stay awake, and we would end up falling asleep. I tried hard to listen to the message that the pastor was trying to get across and apply some of it to my life. I tried hard to change and make myself what Alice wanted me to be. It was very difficult to please her, though.

One night we all went to a church service in Medicine Hat. I had a very bad cold and was coughing through most of the service. Jerry leaned over and whispered in my ear, "Quit faking your cough and trying to get people to feel sorry for you."

What on earth is he talking about? I thought with bewilderment. I tried not to cough after that, and as I tried to hold in my cough my diaphragm started to spasm. So Jerry leaned over to me again and said, "Quit trying to make yourself throw up," with a threatening voice.

Sometimes Alice was not around when some of the kids were doing the dishes, and we would all get along quite well. We would laugh and talk just like ordinary kids. It depended who was present though. Miles did not like to see the younger kids getting along and having a good time. He did not want us laughing while we were working. Dwight loved to laugh and joke with the younger kids. I never laughed so hard as when I was with Dwight. He would mimic me or someone else playfully to make us laugh. He was amazing at making funny faces too. Sometimes when I was taking a drink I would have a mouthful of water and would spray it all over the floor when he made me laugh. I had to quickly clean it up so that Alice would not see it. It helped me forget about the stress in the home. Humour became my coping mechanism during tough times out at the farm. Even after I got out of foster homes I had many years of terrible struggles through life because of the horrid abuse I endured, and humour was the drug that saw me through.

I have done stand-up comedy about eight times in the course of my life. Twice I did stand-up at Yuk-Yuk's and once at the Back Alley in Calgary, Alberta. The other times were in different towns in Alberta as well. Each time I was met with laughter and applause at the end of my routine. When I was doing a job that I did not like I would start to tell jokes to other people so that we would laugh and the job would be easier to deal with.

I also realized that people do not like to be around others who are always complaining about their problems. They like to be around people who are happy and outgoing. No matter how bad things get or how much a person hates their job, they can still make it fun if they try. I have tried to teach my children this and demonstrate it as often as I can.

One night around nine p.m. a car stopped on the road outside of the foster home property, I think because the car broke down. Alice told Wilf about it, and he went and grabbed his gun. We were all told to go out in groups to see if we could find out if the person or persons had come onto the property. I heard Alice call out to Wilf, "Beat the tar out of him, Daddy." It was always interesting to watch Wilf run, because he did not move his arms. He actually looked like Fred Flintstone when he was running.

There were some good things about living out at the farm. I learned a lot about animals. I was taught how to feed them and take care of them properly. I also learned how to clean their pens and barns. Some of it was hard work, which I now appreciate very much because it taught me how to be a good worker.

Alice was a good cook, and I was always fed very well there. I grew a lot after being at the home for a year. The first time that my family saw me they were very surprised at how much I had grown. We had to eat everything on our plates. Sometimes when I was asked if I wanted more to eat and said no, they said it was only because I didn't like the food. So they would then pile more food on my plate so I would learn to like it. Sometimes when we butchered chickens to sell, the buyers would not want the hearts and livers. So Alice would cook them up for us to eat, and it took me an extra hour sitting at the table to eat my meal, because I hated the taste of heart and liver.

Bath night only came once a week, on the weekend. I guess it was to save water. The first time, I was ordered by Jerry to take off all of my clothes and get into the tub. I did as I was ordered. As I went to get into the tub I noticed that the water was very dirty. Three other people already had taken a bath in the water that I was about to get into.

"Hurry up and get in," Jerry ordered me.

"In that?" I replied with disgust.

"Yeah."

I was so grossed out at this, it just about made me sick. I don't know how anyone could get clean by bathing in that water.

We were forced to wear the same clothes for the full five school days each week. Even the night before picture day I was not allowed to wash my hair.

At the table Alice would often talk to the two older girls about their appearance or their behaviour. She would call the girls sluts and accuse them of having dirty minds filled with bad thoughts. She would degrade them and call them all sorts of names. One time I remember her saying to one of the girls, "You have a big butt and not much to balance it out." I don't believe that they had any self-esteem at all.

On Saturdays we did our regular chores in the morning, and then we would butcher and pluck geese. It was tedious work, pulling all of the feathers off. We would cut their heads off and then soak them in boiling water to make it easier. Sometimes it was very cold out, and we would stand outside all day plucking geese. Our hands would freeze, which made it even more difficult to pluck the feathers.

Every spring we would get about 700 chicks and raise them. We would kill them when they were bigger and then sell them. One time Terry was plucking a chicken and he could not get one of the feathers out, so he used his teeth and pulled it out. Dwight started to bug him and made fun of him for days after that. It looked so funny, seeing Terry pulling the feather out of a raw chicken with his teeth.

After they were plucked, Dwight would usually be the one who would gut them and clean them out. They would be washed three times and then they would be frozen to be eaten at a later date. We worked until 10 p.m. most days because it was a long process getting all of the chickens cleaned and gutted.

One time when we were butchering chickens, Jerry was cutting one of the heads off but the knife was not sharp enough, so he changed knives when the head was half cut off. *Boy, that must hurt,* I thought as I shivered. If an animal was maimed or sick and was not going to make it, Alice would volunteer Jerry to kill it.

We also had pigs, and when they had piglets we would raise them and then sell them. Every once in a while a chicken or piglet would die, and Alice would blame someone for killing it, sometimes accusing one of the kids of stabbing it with a pitchfork. She would beat the kid until he confessed to it. Even if he did not do it he would eventually cave in because the beatings were so severe. She would hit him with the black rubber hose or make him run back and forth outside and do push-ups until he confessed.

Once I asked one of the teachers at the Irvine school if I could talk to him for a minute. We went into the washroom, where we could have a bit of privacy. I tried to confide in him and told him that I was having trouble at the foster home and that I really missed my parents.

He said that he had kids who came to him and cried every day, and he did not want to deal with my problems.

After I realized that he would not help me, I went to the school office and asked if I could use the phone. As the secretary was handing me the phone, the vice principal informed her that I was never allowed to use the phone to call anyone. I was very frustrated with my situation. Every step that I took to try and get help was blocked.

After being at the foster home for three weeks something really bizarre happened to me. I got on the bus after school and sat down. As I looked around I observed that most of the foster kids appeared to be upset with me. Jerry stepped onto the bus and sat down beside me. Once we got onto the highway he leaned over to me and said in a very angry voice, "You're going to get it when you get home tonight."

What in the world did I do? I wondered as I started to panic. I thought through every step of the day. I could not find any reason why I should be in trouble. I know that there were a lot of times that I was bad and did not get caught when I should have. But that day I had not done anything that deserved being punished. I went to school, did my work, and behaved.

I got off the bus at the home and stepped into the house. Alice was standing at the top of the stairs with an angry look on her face. "What did you do today?" she asked me impatiently.

"I...I...went to school and did my work," I replied very fearfully.

"Sit down on the steps!" she barked.

I sat down on the steps very slowly and carefully so that she would not think that I was mad at her for anything. To do that was to risk being severely beaten.

She asked me the same question again, and I gave her the same answer. She brought her leg up and kicked me in the back of the head. "What else did you do today?" she asked me again.

"Nothing," I replied as I trembled with fear.

"Don't lie to me," she screamed. "I got a phone call from someone at the school telling me what you were doing today, so don't try to hide it!"

I bet that person told her that I was smoking, I thought. I honestly had not been smoking though. *Maybe if I tell her that I was smoking at school she'll leave me alone.* "I was smoking today," I finally said as I looked up at her, hoping that was what she wanted to hear.

"What else did you do?" she shouted.

"That's all I did," I replied, trembling.

"What else?" she barked as she brought her leg up and kicked me in the back of the head again.

She looked at Jerry, who was watching the whole ordeal, and said, "Why don't you, Miles, and Dwight take him down to the corrals for a while and let him run? Then maybe he might feel like talking and confessing."

Jerry pushed me out the door, and we walked down to the corrals, with Miles and Dwight close behind. Dwight ordered me to pick up a bale of hay and throw it over the fence for the cows. I lifted the bale and tried to push it up to my chest. I lifted with all of my strength and finally got it up to my chest to throw over the fence. Just as I had it at my chest, Dwight pushed me backwards, and I fell flat on my back with the bale landing on top of my face. It left bloodied puncture marks all over my face.

"Get up and throw it over the fence," Miles said sternly.

I pushed the bale off of my face, got up, picked up the bale, and pushed it up against the fence. Then I rolled it up the side of the fence until it rolled over the other side and dropped to the ground.

"Get into the corral and start running," Miles barked.

I jumped over the corral and started to run back and forth, about a twenty-metre distance.

"Run faster," Miles snapped.

I picked up the pace a bit as I ran.

"So," Jerry said, taunting me, "are you going to tell us what you did at school today or do you want to run all night?"

"I don't want to run all night," I answered between breaths.

"Then you better tell us what you did today."

"I was smoking today," I lied. *I better tell them what they want to hear,* I thought with frustration, *or I'm really going to get beat up all night.*

"And what else?" Jerry barked, expecting to hear more.

"Well, I was smoking drugs," I lied again, hoping that I said the right thing.

"And what else?"

"That's all I did," I answered fearfully.

I guess Jerry did not like that answer, because when I ran past him the next time he brought up his leg and kicked me square in the face. I somersaulted backwards through the air and landed on my stomach. Stinging pain hit my face instantly as blood ran from my mouth and nose.

"Get up and get running," Jerry screamed.

I got up, and as I ran, blood dripped onto the ground from my mouth and nose.

"What else did you do today?" Jerry asked again.

"I was drinking," I lied for the third time.

"What else?" Jerry barked.

I could not come up with another lie to tell him. I thought drinking, smoking, and doing drugs was pretty much it. I had not stolen anything or cheated on a test. So I ended up running back and forth for another ten minutes, and then I was called into the house for supper.

As I walked into the house I saw Alice cooking supper. I started to change my clothes, and her eyes caught mine. "I don't like the way you looked at me!" she screamed. She walked toward me to hit me, and I ducked to protect my battered face.

"Oh, you're going to duck, are you?" screamed Alice. She grabbed a handful of my hair and started to slap me on the face. Jerry was standing close by to make sure that I did not fight back or try to get away.

"I don't like your attitude either," she snapped, and then she pounded my swollen face a couple more times.

Dizzy and sore from getting hit, I walked into the bathroom to wash up and get all of the blood off my face. I glanced in the mirror as I ran some water. I gasped in shock—my face was a mess. Both of my eyes were darkened and my face was poked and bloody from the bale landing on it. My lips and nose were all crusted with blood too. I had never been beaten so badly in my entire life as I was beaten that day. The people who beat me were full-size adults. It was my first attempt at demonstrating the ill effects of child abuse.

"Hurry and wash up," Jerry barked at me with impatience.

After supper I helped with the dishes, then sat on the floor in the kitchen and did my homework. *What kind of a place is this? Does the social worker know what's going on in here? How come my parents haven't phoned me yet? Don't they know where I am?* I wondered sadly. I just wanted to get out of there.

The next day when I woke up I felt like a rag doll that had been worked over by a big dog. My face looked worse too. After we finished doing our chores in the morning we went into the house and got dressed for school. Alice called all of the kids to the table and inspected them as she sat down. She opened up the green Bible and started to read while everybody sat motionless.

We caught the bus to school, and I sat against the window of the bus and buried my head so that nobody could see me.

I cried very quietly to myself as I thought about my family. *You won't even phone me, Mom. Why won't you phone me?* I asked as I brushed tears from my eyes. Many mornings I did this as the bus went along the highway. I didn't know that my mother and father would both phone out to the farm but Alice would not allow them to speak to me.

I did my schoolwork and did not talk to anyone that day. I found out years later that one of the teachers was concerned about my physical appearance, especially my black eyes. He phoned Social Services about it. They in turn phoned Alice, and she lied, saying that I had run into a doorknob at home. She also blamed my condition on self-mutilation.

I went home after school and did my chores. As I walked with a wheelbarrow full of hay my foot slipped and my face hit the wheelbarrow. My nose started to bleed, and I started to cry for my mom.

Sometimes when I was doing my chores with Dwight he would do things to make me laugh. We would be walking to the cow barn or pig barn, and Dwight would walk almost as fast as I could run. I would start to giggle as I tried to keep up with him. Sometimes he would fake that he was laughing, and the sound he made was so comical that everyone would laugh. He was so fun to be around.

I continued to get beat up all week long by the kids and Alice. By the end of the week I had had enough. I planned to run away again, only this time I had a better plan. I knew that every Tuesday kids came to our school from Seven Persons, a small town southwest of Medicine Hat. They did not have an industrial arts shop at their school, so they were brought by bus to our school and used our shop.

9 - On the Run

Tuesday finally rolled around, and in the afternoon I watched the clock because the bus left Irvine at about two o'clock to take the kids back to Seven Persons. I was very nervous as time went by slowly. I glanced at the clock and said to myself, *That bus should be here by now.*

I was anxious to leave. I got up and asked the teacher if I could go to the washroom. I was given permission and left the room.

I opened up my locker and grabbed my coat, because it was the beginning of December and the temperature could get down to minus forty outside. My pulse sped up double-time as I walked toward the door to get on the bus. I saw the bright yellow bus and thought, *There's my ticket to freedom.*

I jumped on the bus, and a few minutes later we were on our way. The driver had to go through Medicine Hat to get to Seven Persons, so I knew that I would be in town shortly. But he did not stop to let any students off in town. So we kept going until we got to Seven Persons.

A pretty looking girl asked me where I was going.

"To Medicine Hat," I replied bashfully as I blushed. I very seldom talked to girls and was very shy.

The girl walked up to the driver and informed him that

I wanted to get dropped off in Medicine Hat. However, we had already passed it.

"Well, I have to go back to Medicine Hat after I drop the kids off at Seven Persons," the driver informed the girl.

We arrived at the Seven Persons school, and all of the kids poured off the bus. Then a teacher walked toward the bus and stepped onto it. "A kid is missing from Irvine School. His name is Greg Van Riper. Have you seen him?" she asked.

Fear started to well up inside of me, and my heart started to pound hard. I ducked down into my seat so that she could not see me.

"No…there's, ah…there's a kid on the bus here," the bus driver replied with a calm, slow voice as he pointed to the back of the bus.

The teacher looked at me with curiosity and concern. Then she asked, "Are you Greg Van Riper?"

"No, my name is Glen Boswald," I lied nervously.

The teacher looked at me suspiciously. However, there was nothing she could do to me. The driver closed the door of the bus and pulled away from the school.

About five minutes later as I was just starting to feel at ease the driver suddenly blurted out with surprise, "There's a vehicle flashing his lights at me. I guess I'll have to stop."

My heart jumped and pounded hard in my chest. *That's them. I know it's them. They're gonna get me.* I was filled with horror, thinking about going back to the farm and getting beaten and having to run back and forth again.

The driver stopped the bus, and I jumped up quickly to see if I could see what kind of vehicle it was. As I looked out the window the driver said with a perplexed voice, "I guess…I guess it's turning the corner down there."

I breathed deeply and sat back down in my seat to try to relax. But my pulse rate was still high. I was edgy and nervous as we drove toward my town. *If they catch me they'll beat me for sure,* I thought anxiously.

As we pulled into town the driver informed me that he had to drop off a key at a shop for somebody. He stopped and opened the door to go into the shop. He turned and looked at me before getting off of the bus as he said, "I'll be right back."

What if he knows who I am? What if I don't get another chance to run? I thought. I jumped up and ran out of the bus. I kept on running for about half a mile and then stayed low until it got dark outside. Then I headed over to a hotel to try and steal some money out of a swimming pool changing room.

I entered the changing room after carefully checking to see that nobody was coming. I opened some locker doors until I found some pants. I dug through the pockets until I found three dollars. I went upstairs and got some change for the pinball machines. I wanted to wait around for someone else to go into the changing room so that I could get more money.

A woman approached me and said, "You want to come with me, young man," with a loud commanding voice. "You stole some money from the changing room."

My pulse sped up, and my face flushed. *I've been caught,* I thought with fear. "I never stole anything," I lied.

"You did too! You were the only one around here tonight. Now sit there." She pointed to a seat. "Wait for the police; they'll be here in a minute."

What am I going to do? I wondered. *If the cops come I'll be taken back to Alice's for sure.* That thought was enough to motivate me to run. I looked over at the woman, who was behind the counter. I glanced over towards the door, observing that I could make a clean break and she would not be able to stop me. In an instant I jumped up, dashed out the door and across the street, and ran as fast as I could, with the lady shouting at me to come back. I ignored her pleas and kept right on running.

As I ran around the corner a bus conveniently pulled up to the bus stop right beside me. I jumped onto the bus as the driver opened the door. "I'll pay twice next time," I told the driver between breaths, hoping that I would be able to stay on. I walked to the back of the bus and looked out the window to see if anyone was pursuing me. Then I sat down and tried to relax.

I got off the bus at the arcade close to where my mother lived. I borrowed a cigarette and tried once again to relax. I left the arcade after a while and walked around outside until about 10:30. It was very cold outside, and I was cold, tired, and hungry.

I did not know where to spend the night, so I walked over to my mother's house and tried to sleep in the tool-shed. After lying on the cold cement and shivering for about half an hour, I decided to try and get into the storage room of our house by going through the garage. Nobody heard me, and I slept in the storage room for the night. I helped myself to a couple of oranges and then lay down and tried to go to sleep. But I did not sleep well, because I was too nervous about being caught.

In the morning I could hear my family getting up to prepare for school. I heard some footsteps coming down the stairs. They got louder and louder, so I locked the door to the room. The person tried to open the door but could not. I knew that my mother had a key to the room and that she would go get it. *I should take off right now before she comes back down,* I told myself anxiously. But for some reason I was frozen and could not move.

I heard the jingling of the keys, and then the door opened. It was my mother. "What are you doing here?" she asked, sounding annoyed. "Come upstairs!"

As soon as we got up the stairs she grabbed the phone to call Alice and tell her where I was. I pushed the receiver button down, looked at my mother, and said with panic, "Don't phone Alice! They hit the kids there all of the time. They always beat me up."

"Oh, don't be ridiculous. They don't hit the kids—they're Christians," she argued.

"Mom, if you could have seen me a week ago you would not have said that," I replied with frustration.

But she paid no attention to what I had just told her. She picked up the phone again and started to dial Alice. I sat down and thought about running away again, but it seemed like I was frozen to my chair.

I was escorted to the Social Services building by a police officer. He asked me if I had taken the money from the hotel the night before, and I lied to him and said that I had not. Then he got a little upset and said, "Every time we ask you a question about something you did, you lie. It would be good for you to learn to start telling the truth, you know."

We arrived at Social Services, and I asked the policeman if I could use the bathroom. He sort of read my mind and told me to go ahead but to leave my coat with him. It was very cold outside, and he knew I would not run away if I did not have my coat.

I was taken into the office of Tony, my social worker, and we started to talk. "I don't like being out at that farm. They're mean to the kids out there. They hit me all of the time and make me work hard," I confessed to him. I think this was the first time I ever told the truth.

"Oh, so they're keeping you in line and you don't like that, eh?" he replied. I left with my social worker, and in less than half an hour I was back in my foster home. Miles had stayed home in case I was found so that he could discipline me and look after me.

I walked into the house with the social worker. Miles greeted us both and then took me downstairs. Slowly and methodically he strip-searched me to make sure that I did not have anything stolen with me. He found a pack of matches in my pocket. He lit one match and pushed it toward my face. "This match burns just like the fire in hell," he stated with a cold, hard voice as he glared at me, implying that I was going to hell because I had run away.

"Start doing push-ups!" Miles commanded.

I started doing push-ups in sets of ten.

After the social worker left, Miles ordered me to get my boots on so that I could start running back and forth. I started to get changed, and as I tried to peel off my sock I discovered that it was stuck. I pulled on my sock harder, and finally it came off. I gasped in shock as I gazed at a huge blister that literally covered the whole heel of my foot. It was about an inch thick all the way across and filled with fluid. I pulled the sock off of my other foot and saw two other big red blisters. I pushed on one, and the fluid moved around inside the skin. I did not know at the time that they were from frostbite.

"Hurry up! Get changed and get running," Miles ordered me impatiently. I ran back and forth a distance of seventy-metres again, with Miles pushing me and harping at me the whole time to run faster or he would hurt me somehow. I could feel the blisters start to break as I ran. *Oh yeah, they won't beat me; they're Christians,* I mocked as I thought about what my mom had said.

After running for forty-five minutes I was told to go into the house and get cleaned up. I was then ordered to write out a list confessing everything that I had done from the time I had run away on the bus Tuesday until the time I was driven back to the foster home. I sat and wrote out a list for about three hours. I was honest and told everything that I had done, because they had found out everything anyway.

When I completed the list Alice looked at it and said, "There's still more that you did that you're not confessing." Then she took my list and tore it up in front of me. I was then forced to write another list. I wrote out the same thing all day long. If Alice did not like it she would tear it up and make me write another list. She would slap me around like a rag doll before making me write it again.

After writing for most of the day I was told to go outside and haul bales to the range cows. Alice had been notified about the money that I had stolen from the hotel. She told me that I would have to earn the money to pay it back. Every bale I hauled was worth a penny, so I had to haul 300 bales to pay for it. I hauled three bales at a time about a quarter of a mile distance into the pasture for the cows. As I hauled the bales I could feel the blisters on my feet starting to ache from the cold. I was not wearing very thick boots.

After I finished hauling bales I had to do my chores. The kids were just getting home from school by now, and I knew that I would be mocked, ridiculed, and called names because I had run away. I also knew that they did it to earn the approval of Alice. She positively reinforced their behaviour. As I did my chores the other kids walked past me or around me while they did their chores. When they passed me they would call me names, like retard, scum bag, or slime bucket, to degrade me.

That night at the table Alice told all of the kids that I had lied to the bus driver and gave him a false name. She started to mock me and make fun of me. She said, "Okay, Glen Boswald, hurry up and eat your supper." She called me "Bozzy baby" and other names. The other kids understood what they were supposed to do. They started to make fun of me too. They mimicked Alice and called me "Bozzy baby" or "Glen Boswald" too.

As we did the dishes, the kids started punching me in the arms and chest. They would make me stand still or turn my body so that it was at just the right angle for them to hit me perfectly. This went on for about an hour that night. My arms and chest were so sore after this that I could hardly move.

After supper I was standing in the kitchen looking out the window. Alice noticed what I was doing and said sarcastically, "What do you see out there, Greg? Do you wish you were somewhere else? Do you want to run away again?" She ordered Danny, "Put him outside to see if he will run away again."

Danny told me to go stand outside for a few minutes. They then shut the door on me, and I stood outside in the cold wondering why she would insinuate that I was thinking of running away at that point.

Alice then ordered me to do more push-ups. I was taken into a bedroom, and four of the kids stood watching me. They were all prodding me to go faster and do my push-ups better. My arms were exhausted by then, but I kept going. I struggled to push my body up to do one more push-up, and when my arms were completely extended one of the kids kicked my arms out from under me. I collapsed to the floor face first. My mouth hit the floor so hard that the end of my front upper tooth broke off. I started to cry as the kids prodded me still to do more.

"Mom doesn't need to know what happened to your tooth, either," one of the kids threatened me.

From this point on cold weather and cold drinks affected my tooth. At night when I lay in bed it would hurt and throb from the cold.

That night as some of us kids were getting ready for bed Mike came over to me and grabbed the skin on my chest and twisted it. Then he grabbed me by my nipples and lifted me up into the air. Everyone started to laugh as I writhed in pain while starting to cry. Everyone thought it was so funny that they started doing it to me on a regular basis. They would watch and laugh as I was picked up off the ground by my nipples and held in the air. I would grit my teeth in pain and start to cry.

Every night I had to write lines saying that I would not run away again. I wrote lines whenever I was not busy doing something else.

I was kept home from school for the rest of the week because Alice did not want me running away any more. She also did not want anyone seeing my physical appearance. I was a mess.

Every day I was ridiculed by Alice and the other kids. I kept getting used as a punching bag. I also kept getting lifted up by my nipples. By the end of the week my arms and chest were blanketed black and blue with bruises. From the bottom of my neck to the bottom of my pectoral muscles and all the way across my chest, it was completely black and blue. From the top of my shoulders to an inch above my elbows both arms were completely blanketed with bruises as well. My nipples were even bruised from being lifted up by them. The phone was guarded by Alice and the other kids, so I could not even call for help.

After a few more days of getting beat up I had had enough. I was fed up with getting punched, mocked, and beat up by everyone including the adults. I wanted to run away again. I was down at the cow barn thinking of all the trouble I was in. As I was giving Miles' cow some hay I accidentally scared it.

"You scared my cow, Greg!" Miles barked angrily. "C'mere." He motioned with his finger.

I walked over to him and he reached over to slap me, but I moved back to protect my already battered face. Miles then became very angry. "You wait until I finish milking this cow," he threatened me furiously. I knew that he would beat me severely after he was finished with his cow.

Man, am I gonna get it. He's going to punch me out for sure, I thought with fear. *I gotta get out of h*ere.

"Go out and shovel the snow off the cow barn sidewalk," Miles ordered. I stepped outside of the barn and started to shovel off the sidewalk. *Now is my chance to go*, I thought anxiously. As soon as the thought entered my mind my heart started to pound hard. In a split second I placed my shovel quietly against the barn. Carefully I opened the gate of the corral and slipped out of the door, shutting it quietly behind me. Then I took off running for my life.

I ran for about fifteen minutes across a field to a farm. The wind whipped snow in my face as I ran. It was very cold outside, and I only had on a light pair of boots and a thin jacket. As I ran across the field I could faintly hear Miles calling my name. But I was not about to answer him.

I ran into a chicken house and then realized I would be found. So I ran back out and looked around for a minute to find a good place to hide. I finally decided to go into a building where a big combine was. I jumped into the combine and ducked down low.

I was shivering by now but I did not care. I wanted to get as far away from these people as I could. If I had to suffer a bit in order to get away, it would be well worth it.

I looked out the window of the combine, saw Miles, and heard him calling my name. *What an idiot he is,* I thought. *As if I'm going to answer him.* Miles was pulling a sled. He was probably going to make me pull him back home if he found me.

About ten minutes later I saw Alice drive up in her truck. A bunch of the kids got out and started to help look for me. Mason came into the building I was in and started to look around. My heart pounded hard as he came near the combine. I ducked down as far as I could. Then I slowly moved my head up to see where he was at. He was walking out of the building. As I watched him leave I gave a sigh of relief.

I watched Alice get stuck in a hole in the snow and saw the rest of the kids pushing the truck to get her out. *Good for them,* I thought. *I hope they leave after they get out of that hole.* But they did not leave.

A few minutes later an RCMP officer showed up, and he started talking with the owner of the farm. They took a flashlight and started to look around. But they gave up about ten minutes later, probably because of the cold weather. Alice and the kids looked for me for about two hours. Every time that I thought that they had left for good they would come back and look for me some more.

They just won't give up, I thought with frustration. After being in the combine for two hours I was freezing and shivering profusely. My whole body shook every time I shivered. The combine was mostly steel and held in the cold air like a deep freeze.

I noticed that Alice had not been back to look for me for about twenty minutes. *Maybe she finally gave up*, I thought, gaining hope. *I'll just wait here for another hour, and then I'll take off toward town.*

A little while later as I was plotting my escape route, a man appeared with a flashlight. It was the owner of the farm. He walked over to his tractor and opened the door, shining the light into the cab. Then he walked over to the combine.

Oh no, he's going to find me and I'll be taken back to Alice's, I thought with fear as my heart started to pound hard. He stepped onto the stairs of his combine and opened the door. He shone his light into the cab and spotted me immediately.

"Greg?" he said to me like it was a question. Then he jumped down off the combine. I sat up and looked down at him as anger rose up inside of me because I had been discovered. "Why don't you come into the house and warm up a bit?" he asked with a friendly voice.

"No!" I raged as I jumped down from the combine. I swore at him in anger as I pounded my fist on the cement floor. "I could have gotten away, but you've ruined everything!" I screamed.

He guarded the door to make sure that I did not get away. Then he called his son and said, "Go phone Alice and tell her that we found Greg."

His son obeyed and ran to the house. As I watched his son running I got an idea. *As long as I'm here I might as well use the phone. Maybe if I call the police they will take me to*

Edmonton Youth Detention Centre. It's got to be better than here, I told myself, calming down.

I looked at the farmer and said, "Okay, I'll come into the house with you."

He took my arm and walked with me into the house to make sure that I was not going to get away. "Could I use your phone?" I asked politely.

"Well, I suppose," he replied hesitantly.

I grabbed the phone, dialled the operator, and asked for the RCMP. "Hi," I said nervously, speaking very quickly, "I'm out here at a farm, and the people from the foster home are coming to get me. They're going to beat me very badly, so would you be able to come and get me?"

The RCMP told me that they would send someone out to get me and investigate the situation. I gave them directions and hung up, hoping that they would get to me before Alice did.

I stood waiting very nervously as I looked out the window for signs of a vehicle. I finally saw a set of headlights approaching the farmyard. I squinted my eyes as I shivered and looked to see if I could identify the vehicle. It was Alice in her truck.

Miles got out of the truck and walked up to the door of the house, let himself in, and looked at me. "C'mon," he said with clenched teeth, "we're going home."

"No," I resisted, "I'm waiting for the RCMP to come and get me. They are going to take me to Edmonton YDC."

"If I have to drag you out, so help me, I'll make sure that you get it when we get home," he threatened me impatiently.

Why should I care anyway? I thought. *I'm going to get beaten severely when I get home anyway.*

He walked over to me and grabbed me by the coat. "C'mon, we're going home," he said forcefully. He took me out to the truck and we got in. "We should make you run all night," he snarled.

"Forget it," Alice said with exhaustion. "Let's just get home and eat supper." As we rode back to the farm my body shook furiously as I shivered. I was suffering from severe hypothermia. I never did hear from the RCMP, unless they phoned and talked with Alice or Wilf about me.

When we arrived home I was ordered to go and eat my soup at the table. I sat eating my soup and shaking violently all over. Just as I finished eating I was told to go into the bathroom and get into the tub. It was full of warm water that Wilf was running for me.

I pulled my shirt off, and he looked at my arms and chest. They were covered with bruises from the top of my shoulders to halfway down my arms and from the top of my chest to the bottom of my chest. My shoulders were black and blue as well as my arms. My nipples were all bruised from being picked up by them too. "I suppose you're going to blame that on us," he said defensively, implying that I did it to myself.

I did not say anything back to him. I could not believe that they did not ask what had happened or why my tooth was chipped. I pulled my socks off and I looked in shock at my feet. Every one of my toes had big blisters on them. There were also blisters in the middle of my feet. I had a very large blister on each heel too. I got into the tub of warm water and tried to warm up.

I was shivering so much that Alice should have thrown soap and dirty clothes into the tub with me and I could have done a load of laundry for her. It was just a thought to try and save water and electricity.

"You could die tonight, you know," Wilf said to me as he looked me in the eyes. "You're lucky we found you."

I did not believe him though. *If you hadn't found me I would have been in Medicine Hat by now,* I thought as I looked at him.

"Look at how badly you're shivering," he said.

Well, if I'm shivering so badly and I might die tonight, Wilf, don't you think it would be a good idea to take me to a hospital where I can see a doctor? I thought with frustration.

After being in the water for about twenty minutes I was given some warm clothes to wear and sent to bed. The next day when I woke up I was told to stay in the house and write lines. When I got out of bed I could hardly walk because the blisters were so large and painful. I shivered all day long because of being so cold the night before.

10 - Frozen Solid

For the next three days I was so cold that I could not seem to warm up. I had a shirt on and three sweaters. I was told to not use the outhouse but to instead stay inside and use the bathroom. There were a number of things that happened to me that resulted in Alice instructing Dwight to take my feces and wipe it on my face two separate times within the course of a few days. I was forced to walk around with my own feces on my face.

I did not go back to school for the rest of the month of December. I ended up missing twenty-six days of school that year. Alice said that she did not want me taking the bus because if it stalled on the highway I could be out there in the cold and my feet would get worse. She just did not want people to see the condition my body was in.

Every day I would have to get salve put on my feet. Just touching them very softly was extremely painful and walking became almost impossible. As a result of my feet freezing so badly all of my toenails turned black and some of them fell off. The skin on my fingers turned a bright yellow and then peeled off like a pair of gloves that were too small for me. The skin was very thick and as hard as a rock as it peeled off.

At the breakfast table every morning Alice would look at

me and shake her head. Then she would say, "You could have ended up going to hell. You could have been in a lost eternity. God reached into hell and pulled you out with tongs." She told me how lucky I was that all of the kids came looking for me so that I did not freeze to death. "If it wasn't for us you would have frozen to death," she bragged.

If it wasn't for you hitting me all of the time my life wouldn't have needed saving, I thought angrily.

I lay around for a month with my feet up. I would have my feet up on a bed while I lay on the floor reading books all day long. Jerry would put salve on my feet about twice a day. It took about a month before I was able to start moving around again. However, it took about three months before I was able to walk normally.

I remember right before Christmas Alice took all of the kids to Medicine Hat to go to the mall. I was walking with a limp because one of the blisters on my heel was so large and painful that any pressure was intolerable. The boots I was wearing were too big for me as well. Alice told me to quit limping, because I was only doing it to try to get people to feel sorry for me. My feet eventually healed up completely, and I have no side effects from the night I almost froze to death. My toenails all grew back completely and properly. I can only thank the good Lord for healing my feet and hands.

I remember one day Miles came into the room that I was in. I had my feet elevated to take pressure off of them because they hurt so much when I stood on them. He accused me of taking one of his textbooks and ripping the cover off of it. I confessed honestly that I had not touched his book. He then proceeded to beat me by slapping me on my face, until I falsely confessed that I had ripped the cover off of his book. I could not take it any more. My face was so sore that I said what he wanted me to say so that he would not beat me any more. He then told Alice what I had supposedly done, and she made me do push-ups that afternoon.

My birthday and Christmas came, but I did not see or hear from my parents at all. I did not get any cards or presents from them either. I cried when I was alone while the other kids were out doing their chores so that they would not see me crying and make fun of me.

I was not the only one who was mistreated at this home. Terry, another foster kid there, was a year older than me. He was in charge of chipping a hole in the ice so that the calves could drink the water. Terry forgot one day to make a large hole in the ice, and one of the calves drowned trying to get water. As a result Terry was forced to do push-ups every day. He had to do them out in the entryway. When he was doing the push-ups Alice or Wilf would take the black rubber hose and whip him with it over and over. Each time he got hit everyone could hear him whimper in pain.

One day I was busy drying the dishes and I was the only one in the kitchen. Miles came up to me and said, "You're lucky that Hoopners' dog has a big mouth." He was basically implying that I was lucky the dog kept barking or else I would never have been found in the combine that night. He said it so maliciously to me that it was like he wished I had died.

Because I had frozen my body I was told to stay inside and do chores in the house. I made eight beds each morning and cleaned four bedrooms of all the extra clothes and things on the floor. Then I cleaned the bathroom floor, sink, tub, and toilet. Next, I set the table for twelve people and made forty pieces of toast. After that I would change and get ready for school. This taught me how to work efficiently and be organized.

In the new year my grades escalated to a B average. Having such a rough home life at the foster home worked to my advantage. I was motivated to do well in school because it was one of the few things that I could control in my life. I could not skip out either, so I just made up my mind to try hard for once.

I did so poorly in grade seven that I actually should have failed. But because I transferred to three different schools in grade eight I ended up being able to do grade eight work and passed with a B average.

I did not get along with the kids, though. They had been together for years at that school, and I stood out as a city kid even though I was living on a farm. I constantly got into arguments and fights with the kids in my class. They thought I was stuck up and thought that I was better than them. The truth was, however, that I was shy and had low self-esteem. I would get beat up at home, and then when I went to school I would get bugged by the kids. I also still had trouble making friends at this point. As I looked back at my behaviour later in life I was able to see how my actions kept me from building positive relationships with others. This has given me great skill to create close friendships now.

I remember one time when Alice had gone to parent-teacher interviews. She came home and told me that the teacher had said that I was kind of quiet and withdrawn in class. She said that it did not seem like I had many friends in the school either. Alice told me that her reply to that was "It's not very important if he has friends or not as long as he is doing good in school with his work."

It did not matter to Alice if I had friends or not, but it mattered to me. I was the one who had to live with the people at school all day. The kids would write mean notes to me and bug me when we were changing classes. I just did not seem to fit in with them. This really helped me to identify later on in life with kids who were bullied or did not fit in.

I had gained a lot of weight since coming to this foster home. We were given very large helpings of food at every meal. I started to gain a little too much weight, and the other kids started to make fun of me. They would call me "Retard, the fat scum bag." They all called me "Reets" for short. This was my name for the rest of the two years that I was at the home.

I can joke about it now. Even though I am in good shape I make fun of my being overweight in my past and say things like "I was so fat when I was a kid that I could take the elastic out of my underwear and use it to bungee jump." Humour always helps me to deal with life when things are bad.

Summer came, and the kids spent most of our time in the garden pulling weeds or in the ditches pulling weeds. We worked very hard almost every single day of the summer. It sure taught me how to work hard. I learned how to fix fences, build corrals, take care of animals, and grow vegetables. We did get to go to Calgary one day and shop. It was fun to get away from the farm for a while and not have the stress of working all day.

That summer we also went to a church camp for five days. It was a lot of fun to be around other kids. There was no stress, no beatings, and no work to do. We played a lot of sports and went hiking and swimming. The food was really good too. Alice and the older kids stayed in the new motorhome that Alice and Wilf had just bought. We were in a valley, and they were at the top of the hill overlooking us. I did not know it at the time, but Alice sent the older kids to the edge of the hill to spy on us during the day. When we arrived back home most of us got into trouble for things we had done wrong at the church camp.

I got into trouble because at the camp we sang songs and I did some of the actions and dances to the songs. Alice did not think it appropriate that I dance at all, and I was punished for it.

In the summer Dwight and I played a game when we were going to feed the animals. We would run and then jump over the barbed wire gates to see who could clear them. Alice told us that she didn't want anyone jumping over the gates any more. Occasionally we still jumped over them though.

One time all of the kids were going down to the garden to work. For some reason we couldn't get the gate opened, so some of the kids crawled through the fence and I jumped over it. When Alice came down to the garden she had to open the gate or get someone else to open it for her. Then she asked how we all got through into the garden. The other kids told her that they had crawled through the fence. Then she turned to me and asked me how I got in.

"Well…like…I like, I guess, I…jumped over the gate," I replied with trepidation. (This was how I normally talked to Alice, very timidly so that she would not think that I was angry or being aggressive.)

"Come here," she barked. "How many times have I told you not to jump over the gates?"

"Well…like…quite a few," I stuttered fearfully.

She then told me to open the gate, and I obeyed. Then she took the yellow nylon rope I was holding and folded it in half. She told me to pull my pants and underwear down and bend over. She then took the homemade belt and started to whip me with it on my backside. Over and over she hit me as I screamed in pain. She must have hit me at least ten times with it. When she finished hitting me with the rope she threw it on the ground and then grabbed me by the hair and slapped me on the side of my face about eight times. "That's for screaming when I was hitting you," she yelled.

She then made me close the gate, tie it shut, untie it, and open it ten times for punishment. This was just one more day when I was beaten very badly for not obeying. It was my way of campaigning to become the official poster boy for physical abuse.

If there was no work in the garden we would go and pick rocks all day. If there was no rocks to pick we would haul bales by hand. If there was no farmwork to do we would wash off the sides of the house or go inside and wash walls. Sometimes we would be told to pull weeds in the ditches just for something to do. Sometimes when Alice and Wilf had company over they would make us wash Alice and Wilf's vehicles as well as the vehicles of the guests.

Working all of the time helped us to stay out of trouble. It also taught us a great deal about how to work hard to reach our goals and how to take care of different responsibilities on a farm. It also taught us how to work together with others in order to reach a common goal. We worked every day except for Sundays.

On Sunday morning we would go to church, and in the afternoon we were allowed to play sports. We always had enough kids to make two teams. We would play football or hockey in the yard. It was a lot of fun and let us forget about how hard life was there for a little while.

Occasionally on a Sunday some of the parents would

phone to speak with their children. Alice would be listening on the other phone to make sure that the children did not say something that she did not agree with.

Lots of Sundays would go by when Alice would tell me that my father had phoned and talked to her. She would say things like, "Your father called today, and he was drinking again. It sounds like he sure needs a lot of help with his life right now." She would not let me talk with my father though.

It appeared that Miles was Alice's' favourite foster child and was constantly dishing out discipline to the smaller kids. A lot of times he would spy on us. If we were laughing while we did the dishes, he would report to Alice that we were fooling around. If we were working out in the garden he would sneak down, and if we were laughing or talking he would report it to Alice and we would get into trouble.

One time I heard Miles talking to Alice about all of the people in the house. He said, "All of us are going to heaven, but some of us won't be staying there very long." I interpreted this as Miles implying that some of the kids who were bad were going to go to heaven to be judged by God and then would be sent to hell forever.

I can recall countless times when Miles beat me. But at least if he was beating me then someone else was being left alone. In a way I was sticking up for someone else, so I was kind of a hero. One time I was loading bales onto the hay wagon when Miles told me to get the milk cows and bring them into the barn. For the previous three days the milk cows had been out in the pasture with the range cows. So I started to walk out into the pasture to get the cows. Miles grabbed me, threw me to the ground, and kicked me a couple of times. Then I stood up, and he grabbed me by the hair and slapped me really hard on the face a couple of times. "The milk cows are in the corral," he said to me softly, masking his anger. I got beat up so badly that time that the next time I screwed up and made Miles angry I should have had a credit to get out of another beating. But it would have been difficult to explain that to Miles in the heat of the moment.

I remember helping Miles fix a part of the corral one time. The wind had blown part of it down. Miles asked me to hold a piece of the barbed wire so that he could hammer it to the wooden post. I proceeded to hold it the best that I could, but it was not to his liking. So he took the hammer he was holding and smacked me over the head with it. A few minutes later I had a big lump on my head. He told me to go get some more nails for him, so as I walked to get them I started to cry as I felt the lump on my head.

The next day I was helping Miles bring the milk cows into the barn. When I tried to lock the neck of a cow into a stall it got spooked and backed up out of the stall. Miles and I walked behind the cow and tried to move it back into the stall, but instead it backed up even more and then ran out the door. Miles ordered me very angrily to go and get the cow. I went out into the yard and tried to get the cow back into the barn, but it was too scared and took off. By now Miles was in a rage. He walked up to me and threw me onto ground. He put his knee over my neck to hold my head still, then punched me in the face repeatedly with a closed fist.

When I got up my face felt swollen. I spit to see if there was any blood.

"What's the matter, Greg?" Miles taunted me. "Isn't there any blood? I can hit you some more so that there is some."

I had lumps all over my head and face at the end of that

week. I feel I should take credit for assisting Miles in releasing his anger.

One Saturday all of the kids were in the house to do some work. Miles told all of the younger kids to go downstairs. I was the last one to go, so Miles told me to tell everyone else not to come upstairs until he said we could. I went downstairs and I was going to wait until everyone was in the same room so that I could tell them all at once. Before I got the chance to, Miles came downstairs and grabbed me. He punched and slapped me too many times to count. I got rag-dolled by him and was sore all over. He looked at me and said with a dirty look and clenched teeth, "I'm not mad at you, Greg. I just want to make sure that you listen next time." At least nobody was upset with me for being the centre of attention.

No matter how bad the beatings were, I always was able to laugh when Dwight was around. He would mimic the way I laughed or say something funny, and I would have tears of laughter in my eyes by the time he was done. It was such great therapy for me. Later I would think about what Dwight had said and laugh some more. It was cathartic and always got me through difficult times out at the home. Dwight was so funny that sometimes he would even make Alice laugh.

I was not the only one whom Miles picked on. He beat up all of the kids. One time we were sitting at the table and Miles looked up at Alice and said, "I think I'm going to be sick."

"Quick," said Alice, "go to the bathroom."

"Okay," Miles answered, "but I'm taking somebody with me." He then grabbed Mason and hauled him into the bathroom. As he pulled him away from the table he showed Alice Mason's arm, which was covered with cow manure. Why did he have to make such a big episode out of other people's innocent mistakes? Why didn't he just say something like "Excuse me, Mason, but you have something on your arm that you might want to wash off."

One time Miles was sleeping with us in the room with the bunk beds. I woke up in the middle of the night, to find Miles pulling me off of my bed and slapping me in the face over and over again. I guess I had been swearing in my sleep and I was getting disciplined for it. Many other times I woke up to someone beating me or hearing someone else getting beaten in the middle of the night.

Until a few years ago I still had trouble sleeping at night. Sometimes if I went to bed before my wife and fell asleep, when she finally came into the room I would sit straight up in bed with my heart racing, breathing very heavily and nervously looking around. She would have to say something like "It's okay, Greg. It's just me. You can go back to sleep." Sometimes at night I would have night terrors, and my wife would wake up to find me clawing at the windows and curtains. She would again have to talk me back to bed. Many times I did not even recall what had occurred during these events. Sometimes I remembered when she told me and I was very embarrassed. Until about 2005 I would lie awake many nights, still pleading with God not to kill me. I still thought God was out to get me, as Alice had said, even though I have experienced otherwise from God in my life. But things changed in my thinking after I read a book by Joel Osteen. It really helped me to see a different side of God.

God wanted the best for me and was very interested in helping me to get emotionally healed. He was not wanting to hurt or punish me. I was able to experience more of God's compassion and love.

The other older kids had to hand out discipline too. I remember one time Mason had been acting up and had done something very bad. He was ordered by Alice to do push-ups. Dwight was supervising him, and instead of letting Mason have a ten-second rest after doing ten push-ups he would make him do ten more and then ten more. Each time Mason did ten push-ups Dwight would say, "Ten, go." This meant that he was to do ten more push-ups. Mason started to cry from being so exhausted. He also knew that if he did not do what Dwight said he would be hit.

At mealtimes Alice would call everyone to the table, and we would all sit down to eat. She would scrutinize us very closely to see if we were doing something wrong. If she thought one of us had a bad attitude she would grab us and slap us around. I can vividly remember the sound of her chair grinding on the floor as she slid it back to get up and hit us.

If one of the younger kids did something wrong, an older guy would discipline him. If the older guy did not discipline the younger kid, Alice would hit him or get another older guy to hit the one who did not discipline the younger one. This motivated the older ones to discipline the younger ones.

I was beaten continually almost every day, but there was a handful of days during the two years I was there that really stood out. One time Alice told me to start cleaning the baseboards in the bathroom each morning. I was so intimidated by her that I was afraid to ask what the baseboards were. When she came downstairs she asked me if I had cleaned the baseboards, and I replied that I had. She came into the bathroom to inspect my work. When she saw that I had not cleaned them, she grabbed me and started to hit me very hard. I said, "I'm sorry, I'm sorry, I'm sorry," over and over as she hit me.

"Get down there and clean them *now*!" she screamed at me angrily. "I don't like your attitude, either," she yelled. Then she grabbed me and hit me again.

I finished cleaning the baseboards and then went to the table and sat down. She told Miles to come and deal with me because I had a bad attitude. Miles grabbed me by the hair. He just let me have it. He hit me so hard, so many times that I saw stars and felt like I was starting to dream, but I was actually passing out. I could feel my face starting to swell up from getting hit so much. Over and over I was beaten that morning. It was one of the most severe beatings since I had been at the home.

"We have to keep him home from school today," Alice said to Miles. "He's in no shape to go to school now."

I was really disappointed that she said that. I hated staying home, because all I ever did was work at home and get beaten up. I knew I would have a hard day.

As the school bus pulled out of the yard Alice looked over at me and ordered me to do 1,000 push-ups. I would do ten at a time and then have a ten-second rest. (I am now forty years old as I write this and have to say that I love doing push-ups. I do three sets of fifty push-ups twice a week. I love to work out.) I worked most of the day and also wrote out a list of all the things that I had done wrong over the previous few weeks.

At suppertime Alice asked me to get her a steak knife. I jumped out of my seat and sprinted toward the drawer where the knives were. I grabbed one and rushed over to Alice, gently handing her the knife. If I had accidently tripped and stabbed her nobody would have believed me.

Miles looked at Alice and said, "What did you do to this guy today?" I resented his statement because everything was based on my physical performance, how efficiently I obeyed her commands. I bet he would not have been as impressed if I would have gotten up at a regular pace and fetched a knife for her.

One time there was nothing to do so I went to fold clothes that were in the dryer. I was downstairs folding the clothes, and Alice came downstairs. She started to interrogate me. "Who told you to fold up those clothes? God only knows what your perverted mind was thinking when you were folding up the girls' underwear."

I stood looking at her, absolutely bewildered. I was trying to figure out where that accusation had come from. I had been trying to think ahead, go the extra mile and do something without being told but it backfired on me.

11 - Locked Away

After being in the foster home for a year I started to really get homesick. Lots of times when I was loading hay onto a rack I would see or hear a car coming down the road. I would study the car very carefully to see if they were coming to get me. I hoped it was my mom or dad. But it never happened. I was trapped out there with no way of escape.

Something else also happened after that first year. Jerry ran away. He was now eighteen years old. He was brought back a day or two later. Alice and Wilf took him down into the basement, and we could hear her screaming and yelling at him. We could all hear Alice beating Jerry and then yelling some more at him. This went on for hours that night. He must have been really sore after that episode. He was taken away that night, and he never did come back.

I guess Alice felt like Terry was getting older and more mature so she gave him permission to hit the younger kids to keep them in line, and he really took advantage of it. He was bigger than me and outweighed me by about thirty pounds. Lots of times he hit me way too hard and I saw stars or got dizzy.

Time went on, and Alice became intolerant of always having to police some of the younger kids from leaving their rooms at night. So she rigged up the girls' door in the basement and padlocked them into their rooms at night. Then the younger boys who were upstairs had chairs put up against their doors so that they couldn't get out either. Miles was the only one who was not locked in a room at night. We were all given pails to go to the bathroom in. The room reeked with urine every night because there were four kids in one room using the pail. In the morning we would take turns carrying the pail to the outhouse to empty it out.

I was not an angel at this home either. Many times I became angry or frustrated at the other kids and would argue or fight with them. Sometimes I would call them names and we would have hostile moments all night long or until Alice stepped in and played referee.

I saw my mother and father three times during my two years at the home. I saw them for two hours at Christmas one year, then for two hours on Mother's Day two years in a row. I remember Alice telling all of the younger kids that if they turned on the tears and cried while our parents were there we would be in a lot of trouble when they left. When Mother's Day arrived all of the kids fabricated their phoney smiles and acted happy. We served all of the parents coffee and food, and we were on our best behaviour. I could not tell my father what was going on, because Alice kept a close eye on my conversation with my family. If I told my father and he confronted Alice, I would be beaten when he left. I would also be teased by all of the other kids and by Alice, just like Mason was. I was also afraid that my father would not believe me, like my mother had not believed me. I did not know if my father liked the fact that I was kept out there and not getting into trouble or if he even knew I was being beaten.

As I tried to visit with my family Alice would come over to me and ask me to do something. Then I would sit back down and try to visit again. Alice would come and get me to do something else. This went on for the duration of the meal. Although my family was there for about two hours, I did not spend very much time with them. As they got up to leave I hugged each one of them and said goodbye.

Alice had told us to go and do our chores after our families left. I went down to the pig barn, and as I fed the pigs I started to cry. "I never even got to talk to my family very much," I said to myself as I cried very quietly so that nobody could hear me. I did not get to see or talk to my family again until around Christmas.

When Alice informed me a few weeks before Christmas that some of my family were coming to see me, I stood in the doorway, speechless. Alice looked at me and threatened, "I can see that you're planning and plotting already what you are going to say to them. If you're going to be like that, I'll call them and tell them not to come out."

"Okay, I'm sorry," I apologized quickly. I did not want to run the risk of not being able to see them, so I tried to smooth things over the best I could.

My family arrived a few hours later. My brother, mom, dad, and both grandmothers came out to see me. I am sure that Alice sat over top of the heat register in the room above and listened to hear what I had to say to my family.

They were surprised at how much I had grown again since Mother's Day. They gave me a few presents, then we sat and visited for a while. My mom asked me about my tooth being chipped, and I said it was an accident. I told her it was going to be fixed soon. The time went quickly, and they left. I hugged each one as they went out the door.

I was so happy to visit with them. I did not see them again until Mother's Day the next year.

12 - Tough Sluggin'

My foster mother had very unstable thought patterns and I never knew what to expect from her. One summer morning I woke up in a reasonably good mood. When I sat down at the table I was rubbing my face with my sleeve and smiling. Alice looked at me and asked, "Why are you smirking?"

"Well, I wasn't," I defended with trepidation. "I was just in a good mood."

"Well you better watch the way you do that from now on," she warned.

The next day we were at a shopping centre, and as I waited with some of the other kids at the checkout counter for Alice to come through I smiled at her so that I would not be hit for looking like I was in a bad mood. It worked against me though, because she took it as me smirking again. I got into trouble for it, too.

One time Alice told me to go over to Miles' room and listen down the register to hear what the girls were saying. I stayed there for about half an hour and then had to report what had been said. People were spied on constantly.

My summer seemed to last forever, but it finally was over. I started grade nine at the Irvine school. At recess and lunchtime I would walk the halls by myself and eat some of my lunch. I knew that the other kids talked behind my back and made fun of the way I dressed. But it was out of my control, so I learned to just take it with a grain of salt. This reminds me of a joke that I thought up: Every time I went to school I got beat up. So now my wife drives the kids there.

When track and field came around at the end of the year I entered into all of the long-distance running events. I practiced at lunchtime by running around the field at school. I ended up getting first place in the 800-metre event, first place in the 1600 metre event and second place in the 400-metre event. I ended up qualifying to run in the regional track and field for the 800-metre and 400-metre events.

When the day came for me to run in the regional event I ended up losing. Alice accused me of giving up and not trying hard enough. She could not accept the fact that I maybe had a bad day or that someone else was faster than me. She bugged me about it for weeks.

The second year out there was pretty much a carbon copy of the first year. I was still getting beaten up all of the time by Alice and Miles. I was still having trouble getting along with the kids at the school. I do not know what I had to do in order to fit in with them, but I was not doing it. I managed to pass grade nine with a B average.

The second summer came, but we did not go to any camps. We stayed home and worked most of the summer again. We spent a lot of our days plucking chickens, picking rocks, or hauling bales, besides our chores. I was put in charge of the chicken barn and the pig barn. I fed the animals and cleaned the barns. I must not have cleaned the barns properly a few times because a few of the piglets died and some of the chickens died. Alice accused me of deliberately abusing and killing the animals on purpose. She was very upset with me and went on for weeks about how I had abused and killed the animals. I could say nothing to defend myself. To do so was to invite a beating. I knew Alice's and Miles' hands were probably sore from hitting my jaw. I did not want their hands to get worse so I kept quiet.

Sometimes we loaded bales onto a flat deck trailer all day long. It was hard work and made me strong, but I still hated it. As I lifted up the bales onto the rack, the chaff would go down my back and make me itch.

Some days we would take corn off of the stalks and then boil it. Then we would take a knife and take it off of the husk. One day only Dwight, Danny, and I were at home working with the corn. Everyone else was hauling bales and picking rocks on a quarter section of land that was a fifteen-minute drive from the house.

Dwight asked Danny if he wanted to go do the chores with me or stay in the house and continue with the corn. He said he would stay at the house by himself and do the corn work. Dwight and I went and did the chores. When we came back we realized that none of the corn work had been done and that Danny was nowhere to be seen. He had run away. He never did come back to the home. I later saw Danny in Medicine Hat after I had left the home and found out that when he ran away he had taken a lot of time to get into town. He told me that he went through all of the irrigation canals and did not go up onto the road at all.

I wanted to run away too. "Everyone in Medicine Hat is playing sports and swimming and shooting pool. I'm stuck here working every day. I wish I was back in town," I told myself. I really missed my home and the fun I used to have. I wanted to go back to Medicine Hat.

I would lay in bed at night and after everyone was asleep I would listen to the wind blowing gently through the trees. I would think about being outside walking around with the wind blowing and nothing to bother me. "Just think," I told myself eagerly, "you could be out there right now walking around completely free if you ran away again."

Alice noticed that something was wrong with me the past few days, and she took me with her into town to get the mail. Miles came with us to make sure that I did not run away. "So what is your problem, Greg?" Alice asked.

"I want to go home and stay there," I answered, being perfectly honest. I said that to see what her opinion was about me going home.

"I don't think that going home or wanting to go home is your problem. You want to know what your problem is? It's pride," she replied. "You can't go home anyway. Your mom is not ready for you. In fact, your mother phoned me and told me that there was a group of girls at your house that were your sister's age and they were all half naked and dancing in your mom's living room while listening to music," Alice said, trying to be convincing. "You see, your mother is starting to have problems with your sister. And you want to go back home? I don't think so. Your mother is not ready to take you back," she said with a voice that crushed and cut me. It took away all of my hope of ever being able to go back home again. "You have to get rid of this pride in your life, and then you will be able to live a better life," she told me.

"So the sooner I get rid of my pride the sooner I'll be able to go back home?" I asked Alice meekly.

"No, your mother and I have talked, and she doesn't think she wants you to come back to Medicine Hat to live. She would rather you stay out here."

That made up my mind instantly that if I wanted to get out of that place I would have to do it myself. From that point on I started to plan how to get out of the foster home.

A few nights later I ended up having to sleep with Miles again, and he was upset with me because of my poor attitude. He told me to kneel at the foot of the bed because I needed to come to the foot of the cross. As if Miles knew what I needed spiritually. I knelt at the end of the bed as I listened to Juice Newton sing, "Just call me angel of the morning." I wished that an angel would take me and I would wake up somewhere else the next morning.

My fears of getting hit by Alice had grown to be a major part of my everyday life by now. I was a nervous wreck and was having panic attacks all of the time. Alice would call my name, and I would tremble with fear. I knew I would have to perform for her in some way and if I messed it up I would be beaten.

I was in the kitchen one day and Alice told me to get the silver kettle for her. I was so overwhelmed with wanting to do with perfection what she asked that I could not even concentrate on what she asked me to do. I got a pot with lightning speed, but it was the wrong one. I went to grab the silver kettle but retrieved a cooking pot instead.

When Alice saw that I had gotten the wrong pot she started to scream at me. "The silver kettle, Greg, the silver kettle! Don't you play stupid with me and not get the proper kettle or I'll plow you one," she threatened me angrily.

As the end of the summer drew near I continued to think more and more about running away. I did not want to spend another year at this home. I had no idea where I would go to live, but I didn't care.

13 - Time to Go

One day Alice started to talk to Dwight and Miles about a church camp. They both wanted to go, but the rest of the younger kids were not allowed to because we were all too young. We stayed home and worked while they were at camp. I thought that while they were gone it would be a good opportunity to try and run away. There would be two less people who could look for me too.

Carefully I started to plan my escape route. I knew that there was an old bike by the garage. I also knew that the corn crops were not yet harvested in the fields and that they were my passage into Medicine Hat. I would go straight through the field across from our farm. I would ride as fast as I could and then once I made it to the cornfields I would be safe. I would need a watch and some money for my escape. We were only allowed to wear our watches when we went into town to go shopping. The rest of the time they were kept in Alice's room.

Before Dwight and Miles left for church camp we were taken into town to get some school supplies. I was given some money, so I bought my supplies and then kept an extra $10.00 and hid it in my sock. I also kept my watch and hid it.

I remember it being the last night before Miles and Dwight were to get back home from their camping trip. I had to leave that night because there would not be another opportunity. It was Sunday, August 30, around 9 p.m., and Wilf and Alice had friends from church over. They were in the living room at the back of the house, visiting. The girls had gone to bed and so had two of the other guys. Just Terry and I were still up. While Terry went to the outhouse to go to the bathroom I waited inside. Terry came back into the house and went to our room to get changed for bed.

I stepped outside and shut the big door behind me. I just stood perfectly still as I smelled the warm summer air. I pondered the thought of just being able to walk around by myself and not have to take orders from anyone. I came back to reality and glanced over at the garage where the bike was and wondered if I should run or not. My heart beat hard in my chest at the thought. It had been almost two years since I had tried to run away. I knew what I was going to do because I had gone over the plan 1,000 times in my mind in order to perfect it—or was it 10,000 times?

Do I or don't I? I thought anxiously.

I considered the consequences of running away. *If I don't get caught I'll be home free and end up living somewhere else. I'll never get beat up again either. If I do get caught I'll be beaten and have to run back and forth again. I'll be mocked and ridiculed for the next three months.* All of this went through my mind as I stood outside.

I suddenly made up my mind and then in a split second ran toward the garage to get the bike. I jumped on it and rode over a flat bridge that covered the irrigation canal. Once I got over the bridge I was hidden behind the canal, because the land was four feet lower than on the side where the house was. I rode all the way along the side of the canal to the road. I threw the bike over the wire fence and then ran with it across the road. I grabbed the bike again and tossed it over the neighbour's fence and jumped over. I hopped on the bike and rode as fast as I could through the pitch black wheat field.

My mind was racing. Alice was still visiting with her friends in the living room, so it would be at least five minutes before she discovered that I was missing. Then she would have to dismiss her friends, and that would be another five minutes. Then she would have to organize the kids to look for me, and that would be another five minutes. So I figured I had at least a fifteen-minute head start. I had my watch with me so I could tell how long I had been gone. I also had my ten dollars with me so that I could use a phone or grab a bite to eat.

I must have gone about half a mile when my bike hit a fence. I flew over the handlebars and landed hard. I jumped up and started to run as fast as I could. I kept looking over toward the road to see if someone was coming after me. I was about a mile from the road now, and it was very dark out. Every time I saw a vehicle going down the road I would duck into the field and hide. The wheat was much taller than me when I laid down so it was easy to hide.

I rested for a few seconds, and when there was no sign of any vehicles around I got up and ran. As soon as I saw a vehicle coming I would dive into the field and lay low. I did this until I got to the cornstalks. Once I reached them I breathed a little easier. They were about seven feet tall and very thick.

Once in a while I could hear the sound of the wind blowing through the stalks, and it sort of sounded like someone was coming. I would start to panic. Then I would remind myself that nobody could see me in there and I would relax. I listened to the wind blowing through the trees and thought about the times when I was in my bed lying awake and wishing I was outside. Now it had become a reality for me.

I stayed in the cornstalks for about three hours. When I finally crawled out it was about two in the morning. It was about a five-mile trek into Medicine Hat from the foster home. I was about one-third of the way there.

I got out of the stalks and started to walk down the side of the field. I tried to stay away from the road. When a vehicle came by I would duck out of sight. I did this until I got to the city limits. I knew once I got into town I would be reasonably safe.

I did not make the same mistake as before and go to my mother's house. I went down to the bus depot and waited until about seven o'clock. I got something to drink and then took some of the change and made a phone call. I did not think that my mother or father would want me to live with them. So I thought that if I made some arrangements for a place to live and then phoned my father he would not be as likely to send me back to the foster home. I phoned a cousin of mine named Brian who owned a farm and asked him if it would be all right if I came to his farm and lived with him. It must have really caught him off guard. I told him that I was no longer out at the foster home and volunteered to help with all the farm work for free. He did not have a problem with me coming to stay with him.

I called my father next. "Hello," he answered.

"Hi, Dad. How are you doing?"

"Good. How are you?" he replied.

"I'm down at the bus depot, Dad."

"What are you doing down there?" he asked.

"I ran away from Alice's," I answered anxiously, almost

waiting for him to reply that he was going to send me back. I looked around to see if anyone was following me.

"Stay there," he ordered me. "I'll be right there to pick you up."

Nervous and impatient, I waited for my father as I kept a close eye on all of the vehicles that passed by. I wanted to make sure that Alice was not coming to get me before my father got there.

About ten minutes later my father pulled up in his truck. I ran outside and jumped in. I was very fearful, because I did not know what my father was going to say to me or do with me. I did not want to go back to the foster home.

"Dad, I want you to know that I phoned Brian and he said that it was okay if I go and live with him," I told him right away.

"We better hold off from that idea for a minute," he said calmly. "So how come you ran away? Are they working you way too hard, or what?"

"Well, yeah," I replied, stuttering a bit. I was glad to see that he understood things a little more clearly than my mother had. "They do that, and they hit the kids all of the time too." Then I went on to explain a number of instances when I was hit.

"We're not going to Alice's right now, are we, Dad?" I asked, full of fear.

"No. We're going up to my place," he replied with a tone in his voice that indicated he was going to protect me.

I breathed a sigh of relief as we drove down the road. A little while later we pulled up to a duplex.

"Is this where you live now?" I asked.

"Yeah, I moved last year. On Mother's Day I tried to tell you, but Alice kept you so busy working while we were there that I did not get a chance to," he explained with frustration. I could tell he was upset about never being able to sit and talk with me while I was out at the home. Whenever I would sit to try and talk with him Alice would order me to go and do something for her.

"I know, Dad. That's what I mean. I always had to work and never had time to visit with you or do anything that was relaxing."

We walked up the stairs into his house. Then he grabbed the phone and made a call.

"Who are you phoning, Dad?" I asked nervously.

"Your mother," he replied.

"Hi, Jane," he said with a friendly voice. "I've got Greg here, and he's okay."

"Did you phone Alice?" she asked immediately. I know what she asked because my dad told me right after he hung up.

"I'll phone her in a minute," he told her politely. "I just want to know what you think about Greg coming here to live with me."

"Well, let me talk to Greg for a minute," she replied.

"Hi, Greg." She greeted me with concern in her voice. "You're not going to come back and start getting into trouble again, are you?" she asked.

"No," I answered as I started to cry. "I've learned my lesson."

"Yeah, well, that's what you said before," she stated. "You must be pretty upset if you're crying. Are you crying?" she asked with concern.

My father motioned for me to give him the phone. He talked with my mom for a while, then he hung up and gave me some cereal for breakfast. "I'm going to phone Alice to let her know that you're here, and we'll see what she has to say," he informed me.

He phoned Alice, while I sat and listened nervously. "I don't think that Greg wants to go back out and live with you any more. He's pretty shook up," he told her. I do not know what was said after that. I didn't care, either, as long as I didn't have to go back out there again.

After Dad hung up the phone he walked over to me and said, "Well, I guess you can sleep downstairs. I never had the chance to tell you that Judy and her daughters moved in with me last year. They'll be sleeping upstairs here."

I knew that my dad had been seeing Judy. I had met her and her daughters a few other times at his old place. We had had lots of fun playing games and listening to music. I did not have a problem with my dad being with another woman. He had to move on with his life sometime. Judy is a very friendly, outgoing person. Her daughters are twins, Chris and Nova. They were very friendly to me as well.

"I don't care where I sleep," I told Dad. "As long as I don't have to go back out there I'll be fine."

"Well, we can pick up your clothes after you finish eating," he suggested.

"No way," I protested emphatically. "You can go and pick up my clothes and I'll wait here."

"Why, what's the matter? They're not going to hurt you any more. I'll be there," he reassured me.

"I just don't want to go out there any more," I said with fear in my voice.

"Okay," he agreed. "You can go visit Grandma for a while, and I'll go get your clothes."

I did not want to go back out to the home and have any

further confrontation with the other kids, Alice, or Miles.

That day my father drove me over to my grandmother's place. I had not seen her since Mother's Day. It was nice to sit and visit without worrying about my attitude or my facial expression. I did not have to worry about getting hit or beaten up again either. It was a new stress-free atmosphere. We talked for a couple of hours and she asked me so many questions about life, school and my future ambitions.

After about four hours, I got a call from my brother, Rob. He asked if I wanted to go to the mall and just look around for a while. That sounded like a blast. I met him at the mall, and we walked around all afternoon. It was the first time in months I was able to walk around without worrying about performing for Alice or being beaten.

I walked back to my new home after being with my brother most of the day. I tried to help get supper ready, but Dad told me to sit and relax. Later I tried to help with the dishes, and he again told me to relax.

"I can't, Dad. I'm too used to working all of the time," I said, half laughing.

During supper I felt uneasy about eating with this new family. I had been away for two years, and now I was in a new home. It would probably take some time to get used to everyone. I am sure it was an adjustment for everyone.

After the dishes were done I went over and looked out the window. I could smell the cool summer air. I thought about what I would be doing that night if I had not run away. "Just think," I told myself with glee, "If I had not run away I would be at Alice's getting beat up or doing the dishes. I might be getting slapped around or doing push-ups. Man, I'm sure glad that I took off! This is the life."

"Can I go for a walk?" I asked Dad.

"Sure," he replied, "go ahead."

My father smoked, so there were always cigarettes around the house. When nobody was looking I grabbed a cigarette from his pack and then got some matches. I walked out the door and smelled the cool air again. Once I was out of sight of the house I lit up the cigarette. It had been almost two years since I had smoked a cigarette. I smoked about half of it and then finished my walk.

I went back home and played some games of cards with Judy. I started to have another panic attack. Suddenly I felt like I was getting dizzy, and the first thing that came to my mind was that God was killing me for smoking. I had told everyone that I had changed and was going to be good. But here I was, the first day back, and I was already in trouble. It was just like Alice had said.

I jumped up out of the chair in a frenzy as I searched for safety. Horrified I said, "Something is wrong, Dad! Something is wrong!"

"It's okay, Greg. Everything will be okay." Judy tried to reassure me with her soft, compassionate voice. She looked at me with concern.

I sat down and tried to relax for a minute. My heart was pounding so hard. But I was nervous for the rest of the night. At around ten I went down to my new room to straighten out my bedding so that I could sleep. Then I read my Bible, just like I had every night at Alice's. I knelt at my bedside and begged God for forgiveness for my sins. "I know what the problem is," I told myself with fear. "God is angry at me for leaving the foster home. He didn't want me to run away and come here." My thinking was completely programmed by Alice when in the foster home so I had trouble determining what was good or bad for me.

I laid down but did not sleep. I would get up every so often and pray for forgiveness. Then I started to cry as I pleaded with God not to hurt or kill me. A lot of nights were spent like this. I wish now that my father had realized that I needed to get some counselling, but he didn't. I did not know at the time either that I needed to get some help. I think I needed some counselling. I did not know who I could tell this problem to though. I thought people would think I was crazy.

Over the course of my stay at my father's place there were many nights when I had severe panic attacks. Lots of nights I would run out of my room and accidentally bang the door on my way out. Judy would come down the stairs to see if everything was all right. Whenever the panic attacks would come on I would beg for God's forgiveness. This went on over and over many times every day. Sometimes I would rush out of the room I was in and leave everyone looking on with bewilderment. Maybe they all wished they could have a little bit of whatever it was that I was taking.

14 - A New Beginning

The next day I got up for school. It was now September 2, 1982, and I was fourteen years old. I went to school and registered for grade ten. I met up with my brother too, and we talked for a while. In my classes I met up with some of the people who were in my classes in grade seven. Nothing was ever mentioned about my past and my stealing. I was glad that they were forgetting the past and allowing me to sort of start over again. It was nice to be back at a school and be able to make friends with others. I made quite a few friends very quickly in the course of the year.

I wanted to start a new life now. I was living in a new place and starting a new grade at a new school. I wanted to get going on the proper foot this time. I wanted to prove to my mother and everyone else that I could make it. I also had to prove it to myself.

I approached my schoolwork with less enthusiasm than out at the foster home. There was a lot more to do in Medicine Hat than out on a farm. I immediately grew into my newfound freedom. I had gone from total confinement to being able to go out almost every night. I went to the arcades, roller skated, and played sports, including soccer. The activities I was involved in were all innocent and fun.

I was still having panic attacks. I remember instances at school when a panic attack would hit me and I would jump out of my desk and stumble out of the room in sheer terror as students shook their heads in disbelief. I would return later on after I calmed down. So I decided to go to the doctor and find out what was wrong with me.

So I went to the doctor about my dizziness and panic attacks, although at the time I did not know what they were. I started visiting the doctors about three times a week. None of them could find anything wrong with me. They kept telling me it was from stress. I thought that God was hiding my sickness from them so that He could slowly torture and kill me. There was nothing that anyone could do. God was going to get me, just like Alice had said. These thoughts stayed in my mind and haunted me every day and every night. I would lay awake in bed until three in the morning sometimes, sweating, heart pounding, and breathing rapidly while I shook, thinking that God was going to kill me. Slowly I would cry myself to sleep from exhaustion.

Time went on and I continued to adapt to my new life. Most of the time I got along with my father, my step-mother and my two step-sisters. At the supper table my dad would always say something that would make everyone laugh. He had such a great sense of humour.

Sometimes my two step-sisters would come into my room and listen to music with me or we would go outside and talk about school or a music video. They were four years younger than me and really cool. They were also very popular and had many friends that phoned or came around all of the time. I have always considered them to be my sisters because we have been such a close family ever since I lived with them.

Judy was so kind to me all of the time as well. She was also a very good cook. Sometimes when I was going out with my friends and did not have much money she would slip me an extra dollar or two. She also had a really good sense of humour. No wonder she got along so well with my father.

I met a guy at school named Brett and we seemed to hit it off. He was a very funny, spontaneous guy who loved to play pinball and listen to music. Sometimes we would go bike riding or play soccer or go roller skating. We started to hang around together and after a few months we were inseparable. I was learning how to have fun without having to spend money at the arcades all of the time.

My marks started to drop because I was going out every night instead of staying home and doing my homework. My father noticed that I was slipping in school and he started to voice his concern to me about it. I kind of ignored him and started spending more and more time with Brett. But Brett was not good for me in some ways. I went with him to parties and started drinking again. I also started to smoke because he smoked. I was developing some bad habits again.

After four months my father got me a job where he worked. I was in charge of doing the janitorial work at his shop. I had to clean all of the bathrooms, vaccumn the carpet and sweep the shop floor. I was paid $3.30 per hour. At least I was able to make some money for myself.

I noticed that my father had started to drink more than he had when I had first moved in. It was getting more difficult to talk to him. I was a poor communicator to begin with so this made it even harder. I wanted to tell my father what had happened to me in the foster home. But I did not know if he would understand me, my panic attacks and the anger I was dealing with. I was afraid to tell anyone how I felt.

Many times I felt very angry and did not know what to do to dissipate my anger. Sometimes I would stay angry for days at a time. When I was angry I had a very difficult time communicating with others.

As the years went on, anger would be the most difficult hurdle I would have to try to overcome. My anger had a great deal of control of me, I suspect partly because of the abuse and neglect. Sometimes I got so angry that I would not talk to people for a week at a time. I hated it when people were asking me questions and probing into my life.

My dad and I had a lot of good time together, though. Many times we would stay up late and watch television together. We played cards and worked together on different projects in the house. On Saturdays we went out to his shop and I worked at my job while he did other work. So we got to be together then too.

We had a great Christmas together, my first Christmas with my family in three years. Dad bought me a really nice stereo and a bunch of other stuff. He also bought the two girls a water bed. We had family and friends over. It was one of the best times I ever had with my family. Some of my uncles came over, and we played cards together and told jokes. It was great to visit with my family again at Christmas.

Occasionally I would be invited to my mother's house for lunch. I had an hour and fifteen minutes to eat lunch at school, and my mother lived about four blocks from my school. So I would walk over and eat lunch with her and visit. Sometimes my sister was home, and I would visit with her too. Then I would walk back to school and finish the day.

One time I sat down with my mother and started to tell her about the abuse and some of the things that they did to me. My mom told me to stop, because it was hurting her. I did not know what to think after that. I wanted to try to resolve some of the past with my mother, but I don't think she was interested in doing that. I had always been very poor at communicating with her. She was not good at communicating either—at least not with me. Our relationship was very tenuous for years.

My dad's alcohol problem escalated, and he drank more and more. Everyone in the house started to feel it. Chris, Nova, Judy, and I could all feel the stress. There was a lot more tension in the house than before, and I could not handle it, just because of what I had gone through in the foster home. So I left the house when my dad was drinking heavily.

One time I was having pain in my right side so I told my dad about it. He said that it might have been from something I ate and told me not to worry about it. The pain persisted into the night and I became concerned. I called a cab and went to the hospital by myself. The doctor examined me and decided to take out my appendix. The next morning he had to phone my dad for permission to do the operation. When Dad found out where I was he was upset with me. After my surgery that day he came up to see me at the hospital at 4 pm. He was still upset because of what I had done.

Grade ten came and went quite quickly. Before I knew it, summer had arrived. Dad informed me that he and Judy were going to get married. I had no problem with this arrangement at all. I really liked Judy and her two girls. We had a lot of good times together. Judy was good for my dad, too. She was very patient and good-natured, and you could tell that she really loved my dad and me. She and her daughters got along with my older brother, Rob, and younger sister, Keri, too.

We travelled to Vancouver for the wedding. We drove for four days to get there. They ended up getting married in

Stanley Park. It was a beautiful day for it. Judy's brother, sister-in-law, and children came out to the wedding with us. After that we went out for supper to celebrate.

I ended up making a bunch of new friends where we were staying. We played sports together and sat and visited with each other. It was a lot of fun hanging around with kids my age. The weather was nice, except for one day when it rained all day. I stayed inside and played computer games on a computer that Judy's brother had built. He is very intelligent, especially with electronic things. We stayed for six or seven days, and then we went back home.

I spent the rest of my time with Brett in the summer. We played sports together and went to the water slides. There were many things to do now that I was in Medicine Hat again for the summer. Sometimes we would go to the arcades or just ride our bikes around for the day.

The summer went by very quickly. I was now going into grade eleven. I dug in hard at school and managed to start producing some better marks. I was slowly adjusting to my freedom. I started to party more every weekend with people from school though. I had also started smoking full-time, and my father found out but did not say too much. He smoked too, so what could he say?

I felt like I was getting pulled into the wrong crowd of people though. Some of these guys smoked drugs when I was at their parties. They would pass around a couple of joints, and every once in a while I would try some. I did not make a habit of using drugs though, as I was always kind of scared of drugs. Sometimes I would get together with a couple of friends and we would go smoke a couple of joints together. Then we would go to the arcade and play pinball games for a couple of hours. Lots of times I would get paranoid because of the feeling that the drugs gave me.

I was still having panic attacks on a regular basis. I would go to the doctors three or four times a week. They still said that everything seemed to be normal. However, I was not convinced of this. I had dizzy spells and would feel lightheaded. It would hit me unexpectedly, and I would start to panic. I was still convinced that God was going to kill me or strike me dead, just like Alice had told me. I was still having trouble sleeping at night too. Most of my grade eleven year was like this. I did end up passing all of my classes, getting 35 credits in school that year.

Summer came again, and I was still hanging out with Brett. We spent the summer together again playing sports, water sliding, and going to a party now and then. Sometimes I would go over to my brother's apartment and party with him. He had moved out of my mother's house a year before and lived only a block away from me.

I was still doing janitorial work too. My cousin Blair and I also spent about five days pulling weeds from the yard to my dad's shop and taking turns driving the truck to the dump pile. Blair was a couple of years younger than me but we were best friends since we could crawl. We played lots of sports together and went roller skating or bike riding together. We also played soccer on the same team.

Grade twelve began but I seemed to have more stress at the start of this year at school. My dad was drinking a lot heavier than before. He was drunk almost every night. He would come home from work, make supper and start drinking from the time he got home until he went to bed. Sometimes he would become very angry and lecture us all for hours. I really hated the tension from these situations, and it made me want to escape from them. They started to occur more and more, and I became even more stressed out about my life.

It seemed like everything was getting messy in my life again because I was not working hard enough in school. I had dropped out of one of my math classes, and now I could not continue on into grade twelve math. Because of the amount of stress in my life, I could not concentrate. I wished that I could fix everything, but I did not know how to. I wanted to drop out of school and run away from my messed-up life. I did not have enough courage to go and talk to my dad about the problems I was having, so I tried to deal with them myself.

My attachment disorder was a major problem for me as well. I did not feel like I had a bond with any of my family members. To me it was like I was living with another set of foster parents. I felt like I had no emotional attachment to the people I was living with.

I started to make plans to run away from home and go with Brett to Saskatchewan. This would be the third time I had run away from home since coming to live with my father. Brett knew of a town where we could get some work. He had been there before and worked quite a bit of the summer. He talked about this place all of the time like it was a paradise. I wanted to go there and have some fun too.

Brett phoned the school posing as my father. He informed the counsellor that I was going to quit school. I stole some money from my dad and then packed my bags. Then Brett and I caught the bus to Melfort, Saskatchewan. I didn't leave my dad a note or anything. I was fed up with him harping at me about every little thing I did wrong. I was not allowed to go out when I wanted. I was not doing enough homework and he complained about that as well. I was spending too much time with Brett and not enough time with my family. They were all little things that I could have learned to live with. However, I did not take the challenge. Instead I took the easy way out and ran away from my problems.

I created more problems by running away though. Now I had a father who was angry at me for running away. He would be upset after finding out that I lied to the counsellor at school. He would also be upset at me for stealing from him. It would have been better to face my father and take my punishment for my schoolwork being poor. At the time, though, I did not think about all the consequences of my actions. I just wanted to be out of school and on my own. I wanted to be my own boss and make my own decisions.

We travelled for a day and a half on the bus. We had some stop over waiting periods at some places too. It was October, and it was getting to be winter all over. The weather was very cold, and there was snow covering the ground. I looked out the window as we drove along the highway. I wished that I had not run away and caused all kinds of problems for my family and myself. I felt like I was on a bus that was leading to nowhere.

What's the matter with me? Why didn't I stay home and try to talk to Dad? I could have worked things out. I bet Dad doesn't even know why I ran away. He didn't see any signs of anything being wrong. Oh well, he shouldn't be yelling at me all of the time and maybe we would get along better. I'll find a job somewhere and get on the right track, I kept thinking as I tried to make myself feel better and justify my actions at the same time. Inside, though, I felt alone and depressed. My father had poured himself out to help me, and look what I had done to him in return. I had forgotten how good I had it at my dad's place and how bad things had been at Alice's.

The bus finally pulled into Melfort, then Brett and I walked over to his cousin's place and made ourselves at home. Brett's cousin's name was Trevor. Brett went downstairs and slept for a while. I stayed upstairs and listened to some music.

The phone rang, so I went and picked it up. "Hello?"

"Hello," I heard. "This is Richard, your dad."

My heart started to pound rapidly and I felt my face flush. I knew I had hurt my dad and betrayed him. "What's your problem?" he asked with frustration. "Where did I go wrong with you?"

"I'm tired of you always bugging me about the little things that I do," I replied defensively.

"Like what?" he asked.

"Well, you get mad when I have more than two bowls of cereal. You always bug me about my schoolwork. You tell me that I shouldn't hang around with my friends so much because they are going to get sick of me."

"You could have come and talked to me about them, couldn't you," he countered. "I mean, you lied to me, you stole from me. You want to make your own decisions and be out on your own? Well then, you're on your own from now on, mister. Goodbye." His voice was full of hurt and frustration. He hung up the phone, and my heart split in two. I had really hurt my dad and given him the proverbial slap in the face. I had truly forgotten how good I had it at my father's house.

Brett came upstairs a while later and phoned a friend of his. We ended up going over to his friend's place for the afternoon. I was restless and upset from Dad's phone call and found it hard to relax. I wanted to go back home and start over again.

We stayed there for a while and then went back to his cousin's place. We went to the arcade and hung out there for a while that night. Then later on some other guys came over to Trevor's, and they partied for a while.

Most of the week was spent sitting around the house and doing pretty much nothing. We ate grilled cheese sandwiches for two and sometimes three meals a day, because there was nothing else in the house to eat. Brett asked a few people about work, but there was not much going on. I wanted to go back to Medicine Hat and see about getting a job there.

We ended up leaving Melfort a few days later and going back to Medicine Hat. Back in Medicine Hat I stayed with Brett for about a month. Then he told me that his mother wanted me to find another place to live. So I phoned my grandmother, my dad's mother, to see if I could stay there. She invited me to stay at her place for a few days. I eagerly accepted, grabbed my bag of worldly possessions, and made my way over to her house.

Grandma lived alone in a townhouse on Upland Drive, which she always kept meticulously clean. Ever since I could remember she was full of love and kindness. I had never heard her complain or seen her become angry at anyone. She even looked after me when I was young during times my mother was away.

I walked up the steps to her door and rang the doorbell. She answered with a friendly voice. "C'mon in, Greg. You can put your things upstairs in the spare room for now."

I sat and talked to her for most of the afternoon. I was restless and in emotional turmoil after betraying my father, quitting school, having no job or money, and feeling like I was going nowhere in life. I was also still having horrible panic attacks during the day and night.

One night I woke up and went downstairs into the kitchen. I was upset and crying because of the way my life was going. My grandmother heard me and came downstairs to talk with me.

"I feel horrible, Grandma," I said through tears. "I've hurt my dad, I have no job, I'm not in school."

"Things will get better for you, Greg," she assured me. "You just wait. You will get back on your feet." She sat up and talked with me for a couple of hours, consoling me.

My grandmother must have called my father because a few days later he phoned me. "Hey, Greg, what's done is done," he said calmly. "Let's try to make it work from now on. I understand what you're going through, but everything is going to work out fine."

I felt like crying after that. I had wondered if he would ever forgive me, and I felt much better. *Right on*! I thought. *Maybe Dad and I will be good friends some day.*

The next day I got up and went to look for a job. It was January 1985, and we were in the middle of a cold winter. I went to a few restaurants close by and applied for work, but nobody called me back.

I was still smoking but was desperately trying to stop. By the time the second week had gone by at my grandmother's place I had managed to quit.

I went over to my dad's, one day and we sat and talked for a while. He ended up giving me $150 to buy some clothes and other things that I needed. I couldn't believe that he did that for me after what I had done to him. Deep down I really loved my dad and thought the world of him. I did not know how to resolve all of the problems that were going on in my life though. This was especially true of the panic attacks I was having. I was still going to the doctors and trying to figure out what was wrong with me.

Before I ran away I had been going down to the boxing club a couple of times a week to work out. I had really enjoyed it, and so I decided that I was going to start boxing again. I went down to the boxing club that night and did the workout with all the other boxers. We skipped for twenty minutes, shadowboxed for three rounds, and then punched the heavy bag. I absolutely loved the workouts. I especially liked the fact that the coaches always encouraged my to try harder.

The coaches spent a great deal of one-on-one time with the boxers. Pat and Bill were great people. They helped me develop my technique with my footwork, punching power, and form. I even started sparring in the boxing ring with some of the other boxers. I had found myself a new passion and poured my heart and soul into it.

I started running three miles a day and doing 500 situps three times a week besides working out at the boxing club two hours a night. I was losing weight, losing fat, toning up, developing boxing skills, and also making new friends. I was finally doing something positive with my life, and I felt good about it.

The time came for my first fight, in Helena, Montana. We left early in the morning and drove to the USA. When we arrived I became very nervous. My coach was talking with the coach of the person I was to fight. I piped up and asked if I was going to be the first fight or the last fight. The other coach said confidently, "What difference does it make if my fighter knocks you out in the first fight or the last one?"

I looked down and did not say anything. I ended up having the first fight of the day. My coach wrapped my hands, and they felt like rocks. I got into the ring and nervously looked around. I overheard one of the other boxers from my club say to our other team members, "C'mon, let's go cheer for Greg." I could not ever remember someone cheering for me while I did anything in my entire life.

The bell rang, and I moved back and forth, trying to hit my opponent while avoiding getting hit. I punched him hard in the stomach with my left hand, and he buckled to the floor in pain. The ref gave him a standing eight count. As we moved back to engage again I hit him in the head. Then I hit him the stomach again and then in the head. He went down onto the floor, and the ref stopped the fight after 1:48 of the first round. I had knocked him out and won the fight. I could hear my friends cheering for me. What a positive experience that was for me! I was sold on boxing.

Over the next five years I would win many fights, including the Silver Gloves, Golden Gloves, Winter Games, and the provincial championship. I made it all the way to the nationals in 1987. One time we went to Deerlodge maximum security prison in Montana and fought the inmates. I won that fight as well. During my first year of boxing I also landed a job at a doughnut shop working nights as a baker. Each time I got paid I would use some of the money to pay back someone I had stolen from in the past. Nobody asked me to do this; I did it of my own volition. I shocked some people when I showed up at their doors with money and a sincere apology. It sure felt good to make things right.

I also took some of my money each paycheque and gave

it to a church close to were I lived. My mother had always taught me to tithe. However, I did not attend the church. I would knock on the door and ask the person who answered to put the money in the offering plate for me on Sunday. This went on for a couple of months.

Finally someone from the church phoned me and asked me to go for coffee. Reluctantly I went with him to a restaurant close to my grandma's townhouse.

The guy's name was Sweed. He was about 5'10" and had blond hair. He had a round face and seemed very friendly. All of my defences were up as I met with him. He asked me why I was bringing money to the church but not attending it. I told him that I just felt like I should tithe to the church from my pay.

He explained that the pastor was preaching that people in the church needed to tithe or God would bring in money from people outside the church, so I was sort of fulfilling the pastor's sermon. We ended up playing arcade games for a while. Sweed wanted to meet with me again sometime for coffee or a walk.

Gradually, as time went on, I started to slowly open up to Sweed. We went for walks together and had coffee. I guess he realized that I needed some positive influences in my life at that point.

Sweed ended up leaving that summer, and I never did see him again, but I attended that church for about a year. Sometimes after the evening service I would ask if I could go upstairs and pray by myself. I would then pray for help and forgiveness.

One day at my grandma's we were sitting at the table joking around. I said something to her, and she got up to come over to my chair and grab me in clean fun. As I heard the sound of her chair grinding on the floor and listened to her getting up, I ducked to protect my face from getting hit. I was so used to getting hit by Alice that way that I reacted instinctively to protect myself. It was really a weird feeling after I realized what I had done.

After living with my grandma for a number of months I received a phone call from a worker at Social Services.

"Hi, Greg. This is Greg B. I was wondering if you would be able to come down here so that I can ask you some questions about some of the foster homes you were in," he said.

"Why? What difference does it make now? That's all in the past," I replied defensively.

"Actually, I wanted to ask you some questions about Alice's home," he said. "Mostly to do with the way you were treated."

"Oh, well, okay," I agreed as my guard dropped. "What time do you want me to come over?"

"How about 10:30," he suggested.

I arrived at Social Services, and Greg B. brought me into his office and started to talk. "One of the reasons that I want you to be here is because I have some concerns about the kids at Alice and Wilf's home. Normally when I visit a home the kids are noisy and running around laughing and having fun. When I go and see the kids out at this home, they are very quiet and well behaved beyond reason. A few weeks ago an eleven-year-old kid hanged himself at a foster home, and I have a lot of concern that something like that could happen at this home, because something is not right. So can you tell me if anything is going on? I have here a report from one kid who used to be in that home, and so I want to ask you a bunch of questions and see if your answers line up with his testimony."

He asked me if I was beaten with a black rubber hose, locked in my room at night, forced to do lots of push-ups, and other things that had gone on out at the home. Each time he would refer back to his report and confirm that the person in the report had experienced the same things there.

Greg B. then asked me if I knew if there were any other kids living in Medicine Hat who had previously been at the home. I told him that I knew of a couple. He wanted me to see if they would meet with him. I phoned Danny and Jerry and asked them, and they agreed. So we all talked with Greg for a while. After finding out that Jerry and Danny had gone through the same things, he had us write out things we had personally experienced at the home. We wrote out how we had been beaten, hit, and abused verbally, and then we signed the papers.

Greg B. then got the RCMP involved. He had the kids from the home taken out of school, and then he questioned them one by one. He told me that he did not want the media to find out what was going on; he wanted to keep it very hush-hush.

The kids all testified to what was going on in terms of being beaten and abused in many ways. They were then taken out of the home and placed into other foster homes.

I phoned Greg a week later to see what had happened. "What was the look on Alice's face when the kids all got taken away?" I asked.

"Hey, you just leave Alice alone. She's very confused and upset about what has happened," he replied to me defensively. I don't remember what he said after that because I was so upset with his response. At that time I felt like I was used as a pawn by him in order to protect himself. If one of the kids in that home had hanged himself, Greg would have been responsible for it because he was not doing his job. Here was Greg standing up for Alice because she went through some form of trauma because the kids were taken away. Did he not think for maybe one minute that maybe the kids who had been abused could have used some counselling or professional help? He was only looking out for himself and not the kids. The kids did however benefit from his actions to some degree because they were taken away from her and that abusive atmosphere.

I had quite my job at the doughnut shop and in the summer of 1985 I worked at a restaurant as a busboy. I would clean the bathrooms, clear tables, pour water and coffee for the customers, go to the bakery and get orders, and train the other busboys, among other duties. The owners really liked me, and I got along well with them.

In September 1985, I enrolled to finish my grade 12 classes, but I knew that I would eventually have to go back for more schooling if I wanted to attend university. I ended up completing grade 12 by June of 1986. I was very proud of myself for having enough motivation to complete my schooling.

I was still having panic attacks. Some nights I would lay in bed all night crying and pleading with God not to kill me. There were many nights that I did not sleep at all. I would get up the next day absolutely exhausted. I also had many symptoms for which the doctors had no answers. I thought that God was slowly torturing and killing me. I also thought that God was hiding it from the doctors so that they could not help me. I thought that He was making my situation as horrible as possible.

In 1986 I had insomnia for two months straight. Sometimes at night when I couldn't sleep I would get into my car and drive around for two or three hours. I would do laps around the city over and over. Then I would go back home and try to sleep. Sometimes I wouldn't sleep for nights on end. Then after this went on for four or five nights in a row I would fall asleep for a few hours out of sheer exhaustion. Most of the time when I went to bed as soon as I lay down I would feel wide awake. I tried to get assistance from a psychologist. He tried to hypnotize me so that I could sleep at night. I also saw a doctor about it and he gave me a prescription for sleeping pills. I was told that I had to train my body to go to sleep at night by using the sleeping pills to make me tired.

In the summer I worked at a farm with my cousin Blair near the edge of town picking and bagging corn from the stalks. It was easy work and all of the people I was working with got along really well. It was not great pay but it would still give me some pocket money for the summer.

When I got off of work for the day I would go for a three mile run and do situps to keep in shape for boxing. Sometimes my cousin Blair and I would go out with a couple of girls to a movie or out to a restaurant for a bite to eat and visit. He was not shy with girls like I was though. Most of the time I would make everyone laugh when we were out visiting. I could find something humourous in every situation.

In September I got a job working at a hockey stick factory in town. My father had purchased another vehicle and so he gave me his old truck so that I had a vehicle of my own to get back and forth to work. I had moved out of my grandmother's place into an apartment by myself shortly after I had gotten the job. I was only making $4.00 per hour and so I tried to work as many hours as I could to pay for my food and living accomodations as well as my other expenses. It was still exciting being out on my own.

At my job I would sand hockey sticks all day. A machine sanded the stick but I had to hold it while the sander did its job. It was interesting to see how the sticks were made from start to finish. I worked there for six months and then started to have back problems from the repetitive motion of bending and then straightening up each time I grabbed another stick to sand. I ended up moving back to my grandmother's place after I quit. It was now February of 1987.

Being jobless, I focused all of my time and energy on working out to prepare for the Provincial Boxing Championship that our club was hosting in April. I invited my mother to come and watch me fight. She saw me win my final fight to claim the title as provincial champ. But I do not think that she liked boxing as much as me because she did not say anything to me about winning after the fight was over. My brother also came to the fight and was very happy that I had won.

There were many times that my brother Robert and I would go to the pool hall and play pool or pinball together. Sometimes I would go over to his place and visit with his wife, Debbie, and his son, Robert Jr. Sometimes I would have a few drinks with him and play cards or we would watch sports together. The odd time I would go out to a party with him and his wife. I knew a lot of his friends from high school because when I was younger I would party with them all.

In March I had applied for a job at CP Rail as a brakeman and had been considered for an interview. I was told that I had gotten the job and was to start my training in late April. The training would last for about two months. There was a great deal of information to learn as I would be in charge of switching tracks for the trains to move on. I had to know all of the traffic signals and was also in charge of communicating with the train traffic control person in Calgary to find out how far in one direction we could travel. We would move a train from Medicine Hat to Calgary. But we had to do this while many other trains were coming from the other direction. So careful planning had to be done so that we would not have a collision. I was now on 24 hour call which made it more difficult to train for boxing and plan other activities for my day.

In 1987 I also started attending the Full Gospel Church. The people were very friendly and opened themselves up to me. The music and singing was also more lively than the last church I had attended. I tried to get to church as often as I could but my schedule dictated otherwise many times.

I was still having problems sleeping at night and had very bad insomnia for about two months. These were probably the nights I stayed up thinking about all of the corny jokes that everyone complains about me telling all of the time. I was still having panic attacks as well, fearing that God was still out to get me. It was so difficult for me to break away from this pattern of thinking. I needed professional help but did not know it at the time.

I moved back out of my grandmother's place and into my own apartment again. I was now 19 years old. Most of my time was spent working and trying to stay in shape for boxing. But I was away so much working that I could not get to the boxing club most days to work out. I continued at my job but my psychologic condition worsened due to my sleeplessness and panic attacks. Finally I had reached a breaking point in May of 1988 and was sent to the Calgary General Hospital for five days of tests and thorough examinations.

Once at the hospital I underwent tests by medical professionals to see if they could discover what was wrong with me. I had blurred vision, disorientation, severe headaches, at times it felt like my whole left side was numb and many other symptoms that could not be explained. I thought that I had brain tumours. I was examined by a psychologist, psychiatrist, had a CT scan done, an EEG test done and other examinations. None of the doctors could find anything physically wrong with me though. I was still convinced that God was slowly killing me and hiding it from the doctors. Alice still had a hold on me and my thinking due to her intense indoctrination while I was in her care.

Sometimes I would have dreams that her and Miles were chasing me and the only way I could get away from them was by flying away. I was also very restless all of the time. If I was tired I would go and lay down on my couch. A few seconds later I would be up and moving around my apartment, cleaning or doing something else to pass the time. I was so full of anger that I could not deal with it. I would get up angry and stay that way all day. Then I would go to bed angry and do it all over again the next day. This would go on sometimes for weeks at a time.

I ended up quitting my job at CP Rail as a result of my nervous breakdown. I moved back to my grandmother's place and went into a depression. I got a job at Canadian Tire doing oil changes and tire repairs and I hated it. I had also started boxing again and went to Lloyd Minister to fight and ended up winning the match.

In November 1988 I made plans to go and get my class one licence so that I could drive tractor-trailers. I had to commute to Lethbridge, Alberta to go to driving school. I took six hours of lessons and then did my driving test. I passed and was ready to go to work as a truck driver. I got a job in Medicine Hat moving frieght for Rosenau Transport. I worked there for about a month and then was laid off because the boss was looking for a more experienced driver.

In January of 1989 I went to the college in Medicine Hat and did some upgrading. I did three courses: English 30, Math 20 and Social Studies 30 and got straight A's in all three classes. I was then awarded my graduation papers. My grandmother was so proud of me that she framed my diploma and hung it on the wall.

I applied for a job at another doughnut shop and worked as the night baker until about September. In October of 1989 I applied for a job at Joyline transport moving drilling rigs because I wanted to drive truck more than anything else. I started out as a swamper and would tie down pipe with chains and boomers. I would also hook and unhook winch lines from equipment, directly move the trucks and perform many other duties. The other drivers would let me drive the trucks to and from different rig sites so that I could get some experience. Once in a while I would get a call to deliver drilling mud to a rig so I also got experience that way.

Gradually over time I seemed to get some control over my panic attacks and they subsided to a point where I was not embarrassing myself in public. They seemed to be worse at night. I was still having sleepless nights but not as bad as before. My anger problems were at an all time high, though. I still had not dealt with any of the problems from the foster home and had not really ever told anyone all of the things that had happened to me while I had stayed there.

15 - Overseas

In November of 1989 my pastor approached me to see if I wanted to go with him and some other members of the congregation to San Fransisco, California to meet with people from some other churches to pray for them.

With excitement I agreed to go and made arrangements at my job to take four days off. I was now working in the oil-patch as a swamper moving drilling rigs.

We flew to San Fransisco and met a female pastor named Margaret. We stayed at a mobile home Margaret had arranged for us. She actually lived in Hayward which is across the bay from San Fransisco. The next day we were shown around different parts of Hayward and the surrounding area. It was very beautiful with lots of hills and oceanfront surroundings.

At night around 7:00 pm we met at the church Margaret was pastor of and prayed for other people. Some of the pastors also spoke prophetically to some of the people being prayed for.

In December of 1989 I was at the Full Gospel Church and as I was walking into the washroom I overheard a friend, Barry, say that he was going to the Philippines on a mission trip. I did a quick 180-degree turn and wanted to know everything about it. He did not have any details yet, but from that moment on I decided that I wanted to go too. I had never been on a mission trip before, and for some reason this sparked my interest.

I started praying about it every day and saving my money. I even talked to my pastor and let him know my intentions. He was very excited for me and gave me encouragement constantly. My father let me stay with him and Judy, my stepmother, while I saved my money. Otherwise I would not have been able to go. I was so thankful to them for what they did for me. By January of 1990 I had saved $1,000 and at that point was the only person from our church who was planning to go. Ironically, Barry had lost interest in the trip. As the time approached for me to go my church held an offering for me and raised the rest of the money. They also laid their hands on me and prayed for my protection and success.

There were five people on the team—three people from Saskatchewan, me, and our team leader, Ken. Ken informed me that there were no seats left on the plane to Hong Kong. So I started praying that five people would cancel their trips in order for us to be able to go. God answered my prayers because five seat positions opened up for us to get their tickets.

Ken and I drove to Calgary and then took a plane to Vancouver and met up with the rest of our team. One was the pastor of a church, and the other two were members of his congregation. Sandy was an older gentleman, and Deanne was the other member of his church. We all seemed to become close very quickly as we prayed, ate, and travelled together.

We boarded the plane for Hong Kong and endured a very bumpy ride for fourteen hours to Taipei. Then we refuelled, and in about another hour and a half we were in

Hong Kong. (It is about a sixteen-hour flight to Hong Kong from Vancouver but only about a ten-hour flight back, because going there the plane is fighting a head wind but coming back it is being pushed.)

As we landed I could feel the warm humid air outside even while we were still on the plane. When I left Medicine Hat it was 40 below, and it was about 23 C in Hong Kong. It was even hotter in the Philippines, about 35 C, when we got there the next day.

We stayed in Hong Kong that night. In the morning we went to a restaurant and ate a meal known as dim sum. A woman came around with a cart full of different dishes. She lifted up each lid, and if it looked like something I would like I'd ask her for it and she'd mark it down on a card. I did not even know what most of the things were, but most of them tasted very good. The music playing was very interesting and different from what I am used to. It sounded like a guy with tin cans strapped on falling down the stairs. I am sure that the Chinese find some of our music very diverse and interesting as well.

When we had made our way to the restaurant there were only a few people out on the street. But an hour and a half later when we were finished eating and made our way back to the hotel, the streets were so crowded with people we could barely squeeze down the street. We did manage to get to the airport and catch our flight to the Philippines. It was about an hour and a half flight.

When we arrived I could smell the diesel fumes in the air. At that time there were 16 million people living in Manila. The streets were crowded with people and the roads with vehicles. We were met by two wonderful missionaries, Dennis and Sheila. They drove us to their beautiful home and helped us get settled into our rooms. We continued to rest most of that day to try to overcome the jet lag. We were sixteen hours ahead of Canadian time.

The next day we were briefed with all kinds of information about what to do and not to do. We were told about their culture and some of the things we could expect from street people and what we would observe as we crossed paths with them. We were also given an informal itinerary for our mission trip.

We went to many places throughout Manila and the island of Mindano, helping street people and those less fortunate than us. When we went to Mindano we travelled by ferry from manilla to the island. Once we arrived at Mindano we took a small outrigger boat to the other side of the island. Every once in a while the person driving the boat would have to slow down almost to a dead stop so that we would not plow through a dead swell. As he slowed down we rode onto the swell instead or it came up underneath and lifted our boat.

We went to some of the smaller villages in the region and prayed for the people. We prayed for a blind person with cataracts and he was healed instantly. This happened many times throughout the course of our travels. I witnessed blind, deaf and crippled people healed instantly in front of my eyes. What a faith booster that was for me that God really does heal people. There were times that I also prayed for people and God healed them instantly.

We slept in huts and ate three meals of rice a day. Sometimes we had fish with the rice and other times we just had rice. It was so interesting experiencing the Phillippine culture and the people. The people were very affectionate and personable too. I would go for a three mile run sometimes and people who I did not even know would stop me so that they could talk with me and ask me questions.

By the end of the twelve days I was tired and could not wait to go back to Manila. We could not take the small boat back to the ferry because the ocean was very rough that day. So we ended up hiking through the jungle for eleven kilometres. We had a very heavy generator that we had brought with us to give us power at some of the night meetings we had held. So we got a large stick and tied the generator to it. We all took turns carrying it with one person at each end of the pole. It was a long hike and took us the better part of the day to get through it.

The ferry ride was very rough going as we made our way back to the mainland. We had been told that a few weeks before that a ferry had capsized in the ocean around one of the islands in the Phillipines and most of the people had life jackets but many sharks had come and bit the people's legs.

A few days later we prepared to leave and go to Hong Kong to smuggle Bibles into China. Our flight was about an hour and a half back to Hong Kong, where we met our contact to supply us with Bibles. We ended up staying in a dorm with other missionaries who were also smuggling Bibles. Some of them were preparing to go to other places to preach the gospel. One person was going to Tibet to be a missionary. We ate supper with them and then we visited for a while.

The next day we met with our contact and stuffed our backpacks full of Bibles. I had Bibles stuffed everywhere I could put them to try to get as many across the border as possible. We made our drop in a place called Canton and then went and ate Chinese food. It was very interesting to eat real Chinese food instead of Canadian Chinese food.

We made our way back to Hong Kong by train and the next day boarded our flight for Canada. Once in Vancouver we said our goodbyes and then went our separate ways. What an amazing experience it was!

When I got back to Medicine Hat my next mission was to look for a job. I applied at a brick manufacturing company and started full-time work a few days later. The company paid quite well, and it was easy work, so the days went fast. I moved out of my father's place into a house in Medicine Hat that I rented very cheaply. It had four bedrooms in it.

I had been in touch with some friends of mine who were involved in a prison ministry in town, and they said they knew of a person who was getting out of jail who had nowhere to go. I volunteered to let him stay with me until he could get back on his feet and find his own place.

The first night he came into my home at 1 a.m., and he had been drinking. As I lay in bed trying to sleep I could hear him hiccupping very loudly, and I was not impressed. Shortly after he moved in I started getting phone calls on the weekends at one or two every morning from strangers. About a month later my friends from the prison ministry had another person needing a place to stay. I again volunteered my place for him. His name was Gilbert, and he was a soft-spoken Native Canadian. He was working at a motorbike shop as an assistant mechanic.

About a month after that my friends Val and Howard from the prison ministry approached me again told me about a juvenile from the Young Offenders Centre who needed a sponsor, like a Big Brother, to take him out on weekends and befriend him. I informed them that I was interested and met him a week later. We hit it off quite well, and every couple of weekends we would get together and play sports or go for walks and spend time together.

I was informed by Val and Howard that he would be getting out of the juvenile centre and needed a place to stay. I volunteered to take him in and look after him. He was in grade eleven at the time and still going to school. I did not receive any money or help from anyone, but God always seemed to supply our needs.

I came home one day to discover that all my clothes and dresser had been sifted through and many of my clothes were missing. This young guy had gone through all of my things and stolen from me. When I confronted him, he denied it. About a month and a half later he ran away, and I never did see him again. I believe that he needed more help than I had to offer him at that time.

Another person came to live with me at the house. His name was Steve. He stayed for a few months, left and then came back. When he came back to the house I was surprised to see him. We became good friends and hung around together almost every day. Lots of times we would go for coffee or drive around town and talk.

In September I quit my job and went to college full-time to train to be a paramedic. I needed some upgrading to qualify for the EMT program, though. I took five courses and lived off of a small student loan. I was also playing the drums in our church and was a youth leader on Friday nights for the grade five and six kids. We did arts and crafts, went hiking, played sports, and had Bible lessons about Jesus. They were a great bunch of kids. I started out with five kids, and by the end of that year there were eighteen in our group. I had also started competing as a long distance runner and won first place in the three mile race in Medicine Hat for three years in a row.

I started dating a special young woman in our church, Brenda. She had beautiful dark hair and gorgeous green eyes. She also had a very pretty smile that lit her whole face up. She was originally from Hay River in the Northwest Territories but had moved to Medicine Hat in 1980.

Before we had started dating I used to bake cookies for all the single mothers in church at Christmastime, and I had talked briefly with Brenda. She had a two-year-old son, Joel, from a previous relationship. He was a very soft-spoken child with brown eyes and a handsome face, and he just loved to play with tools. Many times I would go over to Brenda's and talk with her while watching TV. Sometimes we would go out with friends for dinner or take Joel out and play catch with him.

As our relationship deepened I pushed Brenda away. I had never had a serious relationship with a woman before. I ended up breaking up with her because I was afraid of getting too close to her.

A few weeks went by, and then I called Brenda to see how she was. I wanted to see her again, so we made arrangements. Most of the time I went to her house due to the fact that she had a very young child who needed to be in bed early. So we started to see each other again, and then as we became closer I broke things off again. This went on for about the first eight months of our time together.

We broke up again, and I did not call Brenda for about a month. Then one day she called me on the phone and wanted to meet with me for coffee. She said that she had something important to talk to me about. I met her at a coffee shop downtown and ordered two coffees and some water. She then looked at me and said, "We have a problem."

I looked into her eyes and had an epiphany. "You're pregnant," I said, absolutely shocked.

"Yup!" she replied matter-of-factly.

I grabbed my glass of water and drank the whole thing down as I searched for words. My mind was racing relentlessly as I tried to comprehend the impact of our situation.

We finished our drinks and drove back to Brenda's. We sat in the living room and tried to figure out what we should do and who we should talk to. Brenda looked at me with tears in her eyes and said, "This already happened to me once, and now it is happening again."

I felt really terrible and did not know what to do or who to turn to. Here I was a youth leader in my church, a drummer in the church band, and a part-time missionary. I was supposed to be a pillar in the church, setting an example. Just a short while before I was ministering to people overseas, and God was doing miraculous things through me. How far I had fallen from the Lord and from my principles!

I decided to try and run from my problem and go to San Francisco, California. I had intended to go to Margaret Van Camp's church there and work with the youth. She was excited about me coming to see her. But she did not know about my situation with Brenda.

My pastor found out about Brenda being pregnant and wanted to see me. He made an appointment for me to come into his office one day. I sat down, and he looked at me. There was a long silence, as he looked down at the floor and then at me.

"What are you doing, Greg?" he asked, disappointed. "What is Brenda going to do with two kids from two different fathers?"

I did not know what to say. At this point in my life I was still a very poor communicator. I still had not dealt with any of the problems from my past, especially the ones from the foster home. Many times I had gotten people at this church to pray for my loneliness due to not having a girlfriend. I had also gotten prayer many times because of problems arising from being abused in the past. I left the pastor's office without saying a word.

I walked out of the church defeated and angry. I was bitter that this had happened to me. I blamed God, thinking that He had purposely done this to teach me a lesson and judge me for my sin. Looking back though as I now write this, my perspective is drastically different, with much more maturity and understanding.

God did not judge me or cause me to have this problem or any other problem. I simply reaped what I sowed. God looked at my situation the same way He dealt with the woman caught in the act of adultery by the Pharisees. Jesus did not accuse me of my sin, But He simply said, "*Go now and leave your life of sin*" (John 8:11). God looked at my situation with compassion and love. He did not love me any less due to my sin. "*God is love*" (1 John 4:16), and "*Love is patient…kind…it keeps no record of wrongs…[and] does not delight in evil*" (1 Corinthians 13:4–6). There are many other facets of love not even mentioned here that describe God's loving character and how He dealt with me according to my sin. It was difficult at the time to for me to realize this, due to my guilt, losing my credibility, and thinking that everyone in my church was talking about me while running me into the ground. Christians need to love each other unconditionally, especially when we think it is not deserved.

My good friend Steve drove me to Calgary to catch my

flight. On the way I told him about getting Brenda pregnant. It was now June 18th, 1991 and I boarded a flight to San Francisco, California. I left Brenda and my church behind. My pastor had phoned Margaret and informed her of my situation with Brenda. When I got off the plane in San Francisco, Margaret met me with a smile. We drove to her house and she showed me my room. Then she made lunch for us, and we went outside to eat.

Margaret started talking about the teens in her youth group. She said that I would be able to help in the group to befriend the teens and assist the other youth leader.

On Friday nights we had youth group. Another guy helped me with the youth. There were five girls in our group. I practiced some songs on Margaret's guitar that I had learned at Bible camp. That night I played the guitar while all of us sang. Then Margaret taught a Bible study. One night we went roller skating and ate junk food. Another time on a Saturday a bunch of us went to an amusement park. We rode the rides and played some of the games. It was a lot of fun. I painted and did whatever was needed at the church or Margaret's home.

But in the back of mind I was concerned about Brenda. I wrote her a letter to find out how she was doing. She wrote me back and explained what was going on in her life. She stated that it felt like a part of her had died. I felt panic rise up inside of me, because I did not know how to handle the emotional turmoil in either of us. I was not close to my mother or father. I did not have anyone to really talk to about how I was feeling. I never even told my mother or father that I had a child until a month after he was born. I was so afraid of what they would say and how they would react. I was so confused about what I should do. I was terrified about the situation I was in with Brenda. I felt like a passenger on a plane that was about to crash.

I know why the Bible says that "*the glory of children are their fathers*" (Proverbs 17:6, KJV). It is because the father is their provider, protector, and teacher. My teacher had divorced my mother, and I was not involved with him enough earlier in my life to be properly directed at this point in my life. I learned so many lessons on my own.

I got involved with another church in San Francisco. Margaret was good friends with the pastor, Dennis. His church was involved in an outreach known as S.O.S. For one full week we ministered to people on the streets of San Francisco. People from many different churches got together at a Russian Orthodox church and had praise and worship time. Then we broke up into groups and went all over San Francisco and talked to people about Jesus. Sometimes we handed out Bible tracts and other times we bought food for people who were hungry. We talked with homeless people, business people, drug dealers, and homosexuals. We went into a very rough part of the city known as Tenderloin and helped people there as well. It was very eye-opening to see so many desperate people. It was exciting to go to so many different parts of the city and help such a diverse crowd. It was also very dangerous at times. There were drug dealers and drug users around some of the places where we were.

Margaret went away to a conference for a couple of days, and I was left at home with a list of jobs to do. I did some painting and cleaning in the house. All the while I was thinking about Brenda. I missed her and wanted to be with her to support her in this tough time. I did not mean to cause so much pain in her life.

By the end of the second day by myself I had made up my mind that I needed to go home and see Brenda. I also needed to be responsible and face my problems as well as the people I had hurt who had trusted me. I did not want to be remembered as someone who had run from his problems but as one who was victorious in the midst of them.

When Margaret arrived back home I told her how I was feeling. She appeared very disappointed. I know that she appreciated all of the help I gave to her and the youth.

I boarded the plane the next morning after saying goodbye and flew back to Calgary, Alberta. My best friend, Rex, picked me up at the airport. I had spent many Friday and Saturday nights at his place watching movies or just talking with him. He is a licensed motorbike mechanic and car mechanic, and he also builds and flies his own ultralight planes. He is one of the smartest people I know. I had told him that Brenda was pregnant before I left for San Francisco. We wrote to each other and he was so supportive of my situation.

As I got off the plane and walked over to him, he smiled at me. I grabbed my bags, and we walked to his vehicle. It was a three-hour drive back to Medicine Hat. We laughed and joked most of the way. At that point we had been friends for four years, and today after twenty-one years we are still good friends. He is such a great guy!

When I arrived in Medicine Hat I stayed at my grandmother's place again. I did get a job a few days later driving a truck, doing pickups and deliveries in town.

Brenda was now showing, and so everyone knew that she was pregnant. When Sunday came I went to church and sat beside her to give her some support. I could feel the weight of people's stares on me. I felt very uncomfortable, because

I had let down all of these people who had looked up to me in so many ways.

I became more and more bitter. I became a rage-filled restless wanderer. *How could God do this to me when I've done so much for Him?* I bitterly asked myself.

I alienated myself from the church as much as I could. I felt so uncomfortable that I could not tolerate being there any more. I felt condemned and unloved.

I had decided to switch from paramedic training to being a nurse because the burnout rate was not as extreme. I worked driving a truck until the end of August and then went back to college to start my first year of nursing training. I was in classes about six hours each day and spent the rest of my time studying. I had used my savings and obtained a small student loan the first year. But now in my second year I needed a larger amount of money to pay for everything. My parents were not able to help me at this point.

I had no trouble comprehending the information I read in the textbooks but had difficulty when it came to the practical applications. I had problems following instructions and taking orders from my nursing instructor. I felt like I was replaying my life in the foster home and my instructor was the foster mother who was ordering me around. Every time my nursing instructor talked with me she observed that I looked extremely angry. I still had not dealt with the problems in the foster home, and it was now more than ten years since I had gotten out of the home.

In between all of this my son was born. I had terrible problems trying to concentrate on school knowing that my son was soon going to be born. I had not been in church for months and had not told any of my family that I was soon going to be a father. What a predicament I had gotten myself into!

My son was born on February 11, 1992, but I did not go to the delivery. Three days went by after my son was born, but I did not go and see him. I was terrified to go up to the hospital. I had absolutely no idea how to be a father or provider. I was too rough and raw to be loving, tender and caring for my delicate baby. I felt so intimidated and confused about my situation. Finally, Jane, a woman from my church came to me and said, "Greg, you have a son, and you really need to go be with him."

After great deliberation I drove up to the hospital and went into Brenda's room. My son was in an incubator because he was jaundiced. I watched him through the glass as he slept. This was supposed to be a joyful time of great celebration where the grandparents came and held my son as they welcomed a new member into our family. My experience was totally different; it was more of a torturous, regretful time. This was not because I did not love my son or care for Brenda. It was partly because of the fact that I was not prepared for this moment financially, emotionally, or relationship wise. I had gone about everything the wrong way in regard to creating this wonderful new life.

I asked Brenda how she was feeling. She told me that she was a little tired but otherwise okay. I paced in her hospital room, searching for words to say, looking at my son occasionally.

"I don't really know how much I am really going to have to do with this child," I began as I glanced at Brenda and then down at the floor. "I know that God has called me to the mission field and I am going to be working there, so I'm not sure that I will be around much." I was trying to get out of the responsibility of being a father to my son.

"That's okay," Brenda said slowly as she looked away

from me. "I probably won't have time for a relationship with someone anyway. Something tells me that I'll be too busy taking care of two little boys."

As I write this sixteen years later I abhor my selfishness. I still have trouble forgiving myself for what I said to her and how I treated her and our son, whom we had decided together to name Roman. Even now there is no comfort to ease the pain of this memory. Brenda was prepared at this point to give up her whole life to take care of her children, and I was bailing out of the responsibility faster than a guy with a parachute jumping out of a plane on fire. I was very confused. I did not know if I really loved Brenda or not. I was not really sure what love was or what it meant to be in love.

My attachment disorder was shining through again. The people who were closest to me in my past and had said they loved me had abandoned me or beaten me.

During my time at the Medicine Hat College I had been eating protein supplements and going to the gym and lifting weights for two hours every day. I had added a significant amount of muscle to my frame. I had also become more angry and bitter about the way my life had gone, thinking that I was a victim, with God making these things happen to me, instead of accepting the fact that I had made poor decisions and was ultimately to blame for the way things had gone. I was reaping what I had sowed.

At the end of my third semester of the nursing program I had managed to pass everything, but I could not find a job. It was late in June when I went to look for work. I ended up taking a job at a service station pumping gas. I made very little money but still gave Brenda money every month to help her with the bills.

Once in a while I would go over to Brenda's place to see

Roman. I would lift him up very high over my head, and he would grin ear to ear. I felt an immediate attachment to him. I talked with Brenda to find out how things were going with her. Out conversation was limited to intermittent small talk. Brenda had been working as a legal secretary at a lawyer's office and loved her job. It must have been very difficult for her, because she was forced to quit to care for Joel and Roman. I also started dating another woman I had met at a restaurant. We started to see each other almost every day. But when we were together I felt guilty about being with her instead of Brenda. We also fought a lot with each other.

The summer flew by, and I started my second year of nursing. By the third week of school I was in trouble with the instructors. I was not following instructions properly, and I always seemed angry. The instructors called me into a meeting and told me that if I did not resign from the program they would be forced to kick me out of it. With tears in my eyes I left the college campus. I felt like such a failure at everything that I did. I was very ashamed about my whole life and the way things had gone.

At this point I had no job, no money, no place to live, and a son to support. I never did tell anyone the real reason that I left the nursing program. I lied and said that it was because I did not like the practical work involved. I believe that if I had been able to resolve some of the problems that plagued me from the foster home I would have been more successful at the nursing program. I had so many problems from my past that needed repairing that I could not progress with my life properly and be the person that I needed to be.

I left Medicine Hat and drove to Edmonton to start

working on the drilling rigs. I worked there for two weeks and absolutely hated it. I headed back to Medicine Hat to see if I could get a job there. It was now November of 1992. I had to go to Social Services to get help from them so that I could at least have a place to sleep at night. They found me a duplex where two women were living. My car broke down a few days later and I had no money to fix it. So I had no way to get to work even if I got a job. I went into a deep depression as a result of my misfortune.

I still had a great deal of bitterness against God and did not want to go to church. But I kept praying that God would keep my heart soft through all of my circumstances. In spite of my anger and bitterness (and immaturity as a Christian), I started attending the Victory church. They did not have a drummer, and so I told the band leader that I had played the drums. He asked if I would be willing to play on Sundays, and I humbly agreed to.

On Friday nights I went to the youth group and started to get involved with the teens. I told the youth leader that I just wanted to come and help out with whatever they needed and that I was not looking for a position of any sort. I wanted to work behind the scenes. We prayed for the teenagers who were having problems or needed help in some particular area of their lives. Sometimes we would go skating or just for coffee and talk. It was a lot of fun and made me feel good that I was able to help others who were in need.

The senior pastor, Roy, asked me one day if I would like to go with a couple of other people from our church to Etzicom to lead praise and worship and play my guitar. I told him that I would love to, and so one Sunday we packed up and went to Etzicom. It made me feel good that the pastor had trusted me. I really did love the Lord and wanted to serve Him with my whole heart. I broke up with the woman I had been seeing as I attempted to rid my life of extraneous things that were causing me stress and distraction. I wanted to have time to think clearly.

Time rolled by, and in September of 1993 I was working at a gravel crusher in McGrath just outside of Lethbridge, Alberta. I was still running three miles a day. As I ran I thought about Brenda, Joel and Roman. I wondered where would we all be in ten years as I looked ahead to 2003. I really examined my heart, because I did not want to make more mistakes or miss out on the opportunity to be a part of Brenda's, Joel's, and Roman's lives. I wanted to be with them, but I did not know if I was ready for a lifetime commitment to them. Brenda was a woman with many great qualities. She had a real softness in her personality that drew me to her. She was very pretty, soft-spoken and gentle. She loved the Lord with all of her heart and was very intelligent.

When I got back to Medicine Hat on my days off I decided to take a chance and call her. I asked if she wanted to go for coffee, and so we met at a restaurant to talk.

"How is everything going?" I asked.

"Not bad," she answered. "Life has been interesting, to say the least. It has been a challenge taking care of two boys."

"How is everyone at church doing?" I asked, looking away nervously.

"Good," she replied, "Not much has changed."

I really wanted to make things work with Brenda. But I did not want to start going out with her again and then break up with her. I knew that if I was to start dating her again it would ultimately lead to marriage. I did not know if I was ready to make that kind of a commitment to her.

Many nights I had lain awake for hours thinking about this moment. Other nights I had gotten into my car and driven miles and miles as I deliberated what to do. I missed Brenda very much, but I was unsure of committing my whole life to her.

"Brenda, I do want to start seeing you again," I informed her softly.

There was a long silence, and I was afraid of what she might say to me.

"Okay," she finally began, "but I'm only going to take you back one more time."

I had been given an ultimatum, and I could not blow it. I wanted to make sure that I did things properly this time. I prayed hard that I would be given wisdom to make good decisions and have stability in my thinking. I also kept praying that God would keep my heart soft.

I believed that Brenda and I could make our relationship work despite the problems we had been through and we had to stay positive. My pastor, Ron, used to say, "Some people are so negative, if you put them in a dark room they would develop."

In October 2003 we started dating again. Sometimes we would meet for lunch at the place I was renting and eat mushroom soup together. It was something we both loved. Sometimes I would go over to her place to visit Roman and Joel. As our relationship deepened I became more serious about marriage and spending my life with Brenda, Joel and Roman.

16 - Just Married

I was saving my money to purchase an engagement ring for Brenda. After I had gotten the ring for her I planned an evening to present it to her. We went for a walk and then I stopped her. I got down on one knee as I proposed to Brenda, and she accepted my proposal with a smile. We were married on May 14, 1994. God showed a great deal of kindness and generosity to us as He provided for us through other people. Brenda's mother paid to rent her a wedding dress and also helped organize the wedding and made the decorations. Other people cooked a turkey or ham for us and helped to decorate the hall. I picked Rex as my best man, and Brenda picked Shelly, her best friend for years and years, as her maid of honour. I was also very good friends with Shelley's husband, Ron, who has a great sense of humour. Keith, another good friend, was the master of ceremonies, and he did a fantastic job.

Our families and friends all came to the wedding, and everyone had a great time. Brenda's stepmother brought a pinata for the kids. When the children finally broke it open, piles of candy and rubber balls fell out of it. We set up a wishing well for money instead of gifts but received both anyway. After the wedding some friends of ours took pictures for us. Tony took better pictures of us than the professional photographer we had hired.

Brenda and I went to Mexico for two weeks and stayed at her father's place. It was great to get away by ourselves without the kids. Brenda's brother John looked after Joel and Roman for the two weeks. He also built me a car out of two other vehicles as a wedding present. John is an amazing self-taught mechanic, machinist, and welder.

The most fulfilling times I have ever had in my life have been with my darling wife and two kids. I have been enriched in so many ways due to my relationship with them. They have taught me so many things about life. It has been challenging but also such a great honour providing and caring for my family in many ways. That is by far the greatest ministry I will ever be given from God.

When we arrived back in Medicine Hat I starting driving a truck again in the oil patch on twenty-four-hour call. The pay was not very good, and I did not enjoy working through the night. I switched jobs and started driving a gravel truck in Brooks, Alberta. It was an hour drive from Medicine Hat and long days, but it was better pay. I worked there until the end of November and then got laid off. I collected unemployment insurance for the winter, and then in March I went back and drove a gravel truck in Brooks again for a different company.

I really enjoyed working there, but the place I was working at now was an hour and a half drive from Medicine Hat, so I stayed with my cousin Blair in Brooks, only a half-hour drive from work. Brenda and I started talking about moving to Brooks, but she wanted me to work at my job for three months before we committed to moving there.

Vacancies in Brooks were almost at zero because it was

an oil town and at that point production was at an all-time high. Every Wednesday the newspaper would come out and I would look for places to rent. I finally found one and put a $630 deposit on the place. We then put a deposit on a moving truck to move on May 31, 1995.

The day before we were supposed to move my boss called me into his office and informed me that the company was switching from building rig pads to only hauling gravel and so I was only going to get a few days of work per week. *Now what am I going to do?* I thought anxiously. *I just put out all of this money to move, and now everything has fallen through for me.*

I phoned Brenda the first chance I had and told her what had happened. I told her that I felt we should still move because there were lots of jobs in Brooks and I would be able to find something else. So the next day I went back to Medicine Hat and we loaded up the moving van. Brenda had packed everything in the house by herself. I thank God that my wife is such a hard worker.

By the end of the next day we were moved into our new home. But I did not end up working very much in June. When I got paid I did not even have enough money to pay our rent, let alone for groceries or the power bill. What a situation we were in!

In July I decided to look for a better job that paid more money. I dropped off resumes at five or six places. I received a call from one trucking company who wanted me to come in immediately for an interview. They hired me on the spot and told me that I was to start my training the next day. I would be driving a truck with a trailer and hauling oil.

The next day I started my two weeks of training. I got up early and worked long hours every day. But after being there a month I did not make very much money. The company I was working for underbid many other companies to get more work. I was being paid a percentage of what the truck made. So by the time I calculated how much money I had made it added up to about three or four dollars per hour.

I was very discouraged when I took my pay home and talked to Brenda. My pay was less than when I had worked hauling gravel two or three days per week. So I decided to go back to my old job and haul gravel. At least I was getting my money's worth for the hours I put in. My uncle Brian told me that he worked with a guy who used to say, "I had better take my cheque to the bank because it is too small to make it there on its own."

My wife, children, and I started attending the Victory church in Brooks shortly after we moved there. I really enjoyed the praise and worship music. It was hard to get to know people, though. Brooks was a very transient city, and so people were always coming and going.

One day someone at the church told me that the trucking company he worked for was looking for drivers. I got excited as I thought about finding a better job with more hours. I found out the name of the company and applied there the next day. I ended up getting hired a short time later. I worked twenty-seven days on and four off with an average of 100 hours per week. I was finally making better money with more hours. I worked there for five years, hauling all kinds of fluids in the oil patch.

The company treated me very well. They had a dental plan, so we could get our teeth fixed and cleaned. Every spring they would have a steak barbeque. In the fall they had a corn roast, and everyone played sports together.

Then at Christmas they had a party for the kids and then another one on another night for the adults. They would buy all kinds of expensive gifts and then have draws for them.

In 1995 after I started at my new job my wife read an ad in the newspaper that some people who went to the United States every winter were looking for someone to housesit for them. It was a rent-free deal for six months. We would only be required to pay the gas bill. Brenda and I jumped at the chance. We thought it would be a great way to save money to buy a house. So we moved once again in the middle of October out to an acreage about a twenty minute drive from Brooks.

Our older son, Joel, had to catch a bus to get to school from there. Brenda would drive him to the bus stop and wait for the bus with him. I saw so little of my kids the first year I worked in Brooks that when I had my four days off I took Joel out of school so that I could spend some time with him. We rented a bunch of cartoon movies and ate junk food for two days. It was so much fun.

Brenda and I asked a real estate agent to find us a house in Brooks for under $100,000. He looked for about two months and finally found one. By that time we had saved up almost enough money for our down payment. Brenda's father gave us some extra money to help us out. We finally purchased our first house and on April 15th, 1996, we moved in.

We had to live in the basement for the first three months because the upstairs needed a considerable amount of work. We painted the ceilings with a coat of white paint, and then my father volunteered to do a second coat. We mudded and sanded all of the bedrooms. Then we painted the walls, and the rooms looked like they were brand new. Brenda's mother and brother came to the house and helped paint and mud the walls along with many other chores.

That spring after the house renovations were done I built an 8'x8' tree house that was raised 5' off of the ground. There were steps leading up to the door and a shuttered window. I also put a spindle railing all the way around the porch. It had a peaked roof with shingles. My wife painted the whole thing by herself. My kids just loved it, and so did their friends. We played cops and robbers in it, had water balloon fights, and even had sleepovers in it. It was a great investment for recreational purposes.

One time I went up to Calgary to do stand-up comedy at Yuk Yuk's at the Blackfoot Inn. I loved to make people laugh and had done stand-up about three times prior to this. I entered into a contest for Canada's funniest comic. I wrote all of my own material for the show.

When my time came to be on stage I said my jokes and had a great response with a lot of laughs from the audience. I did not win, but it was great fun telling my jokes.

But all was not well with our family. There was a monster living inside of me that unleashed itself whenever a situation arose that did not go my way. I would yell and pound my fists as I tormented everyone in my family with my fits of anger. My children were afraid of me, and it drove Brenda and I apart. I did not know how to control my anger. I had still not dealt with my problems from the foster home, either. I was still very angry from being beaten and mistreated, but I did not know how to go about getting help. At that point I did not know that the things I had endured in the foster home were causing me to have trouble coping with life issues. I just thought I was a guy with a bad temper. Many more years would go by before I would recieve help for my problems. This caused untold grief for my family and I.

I was still exercising and running three miles a day. But I had been reading about a contest called a triathlon. I had decided that I wanted to try competing in one. So I started training and running six miles a day. Then I worked my way up to running twelve miles twice a week. I could not run that distance more than twice a week, because I became too tired. I also started biking about thirty kilometres twice a week. But work picked up and I ended up driving fourteen to seventeen hours per day again, so I had to stop training so hard.

After working in Brooks for five years and being gone so much, I decided that it was time to look for a different job. Brenda had not worked during those five years. We thought it was much more important for her to be home with the kids and nurture them. I believe it was worth it and paid off for our kids in the long run. They had so much more security due to Brenda always being there for them.

It was now March of 2000. My oldest son, Joel, was eleven, and my younger son, Roman, was eight. They were both doing very well in school and proved to be intelligent kids. Joel was an honour student in his first five years of school. Roman had only finished up to grade two, and he also had very high marks.

I started looking for other work in the newspapers and the employment office computer job search files. After weeks of looking I finally found a job that seemed worthy to pursue, becoming a subcontractor for a courier company in Calgary.

I called the contact person, Rob, about the job and set up an appointment. Brenda went with me to help me make a proper evaluation of the job. After talking with Rob we felt very comfortable pursuing the job. I had to purchase a cargo van and be ready to go to work on March 20, 2000, in Calgary. We went shopping for a van the next day. A few days later I had purchased a cargo van for my new venture. I showed up at the Calgary Airport at five in the morning and prepared for my first day as a courier.

It was very confusing for the bosses at first as they tried to figure out who was to deliver certain packages in each different zone of southern Alberta. The contract couriers did not deliver in the city of Calgary. We delivered to the acreages and small towns outside of Calgary, from Red Deer south to the border of Canada. It was a huge area that my bosses had taken over. But after a few weeks things were running very smoothly as the bosses progressed with organizing the routes.

I had to stay with Randy, a friend in Calgary from Monday to Friday while I worked, and then I would go home each weekend. Brenda and I talked about moving to Calgary, but she wanted me to try the job for three months before moving.

I came home one Friday night for the weekend, and the next morning Brenda and I got up to plan our day. We would usually get up and have coffee together for an hour and talk. We began to plan what we needed to do to fix our house so that we could sell it and move.

At about 10 a.m. the phone rang, so I got up and answered it. It was my brother-in-law, Dean, from Medicine Hat.

"Hi, Greg," came the voice from the other end. "Your dad just died."

"What?" I answered in disbelief.

"Your dad just died," Dean repeated.

"How did he die?"

"He just died of a heart attack," replied Dean, almost whispering.

"Okay. Thanks for the call," I said back to him.

I hung up the phone and looked over at Brenda. "My dad just died," I said, in shock.

Brenda asked me if I wanted to go to Medicine Hat to see my family, and I told her that I needed to stay home and work on the house while I tried to absorb what had just happened. So we stayed home and worked on the house. I went into my room later that night and cried by myself where nobody could see me. "Dad," I said to myself as I wept. There were so many things I wanted to do with my father and so many things I wanted to tell him.

The next day we drove to Medicine Hat to see my stepmother and the rest of my family. We bought flowers for my grandmother and stepmom. I walked into the house, and my stepmother, Judy, was at the top of the stairs. She looked at me with such hopelessness in her face, I went and hugged her right away. We visited with my sister, brother, and two stepsisters most of the afternoon as we tried to comfort each other.

I phoned my boss and told him what had happened. I explained to him that I would need to take a day off so that I could attend my father's funeral. He was very understanding and gave me a few paid days off.

For the funeral I wrote down all of the good memories I had of my father. I went up to the front and read the list to everyone present. It was a very difficult day for everyone, especially my stepmother.

I did not sleep for about a month after my father died. I had always wanted to go golfing with him just one time, but it was not to be. Many times when I was younger, around 1993, I would phone him up and ask him if I could take him out for breakfast or golfing, and he would always decline my invitation. It got to the point that I told myself that I would never ask him to do anything with me again because I could not endure him saying no to me.

About a year after my dad died I found out that he had gone golfing with my brothers-in-law. Perhaps he did not want to go golfing with me because he felt guilty about sending me to the foster homes. I guess I will never know the reason why. But I was thankful for all of the good times I had been able to spend with him. Whenever I think of my dad now I always recall his laughter and great sense of humour that has inspired me in so many ways.

Life marched on as Brenda and I made plans to move to Calgary. We put our house up for sale in May so that we could move in July. I went back to work in Calgary, attempting to improve life for my family. Many times I would be doing my courier route and thoughts of my father would enter my mind while tears came to my eyes. I missed him so much.

One day one of my bosses was voicing his frustration about one of the other couriers. "Are you looking for another driver?" I asked.

"I might be," he replied.

"Well, I could get my wife to fill a position if you need another driver," I volunteered.

"I'll keep that in mind," he said.

I called my wife later that night and told her about it. She was excited about the job but also very guarded. "I don't want to be working and not be able to take care of the kids or other things that need my attention," she warned me. "I also do not want to work for more than a year at that job."

A buyer for our house had come forward. He put a down

payment on our house with some conditions. One of them was that we get rid of the tree house. We were excited about selling our house for $117,000 since we had bought it for $90,000. I offered the tree house to my cousin. One day he came over and we disassembled it to the point that he was able to load it on a trailer and move it.

Every night after work in Calgary I would go with a real estate agent to look at houses in Airdrie. We didn't want a house on a main drag or close to railroad tracks. After weeks of searching we finally found one suitable for us.

Brenda had been packing all of our things in Brooks. On the weekend I came home, mowed the lawn, and took care of any last minute chores. We put our beloved dog, Princess Dakota, into a kennel for a week while we moved into our new house. The possession date was July 21, 2000, but we had to be out of our home before July 1 because the person who purchased it wanted to move in on that date. We arranged to rent a condo for three weeks in Airdrie until we could move into our new home. Brenda had also been awarded the route my boss had been talking about, so we purchased another van for her.

As we were getting ready to leave Brooks we got a phone call. Our real estate agent in Airdrie informed us that we would have to get the money for the down payment on our new house from another source, because the person who had purchased our house had backed out of the deal and wanted his down payment back.

Brenda and I were livid. We had already put out $500 for renting the moving truck and $1,500 to rent the condo. We had also been charged a prorate for the last thirteen days of the house payment in July. We ended up having to borrow the money for the down payment from Brenda's stepfather.

In the end we had lost $10,000 on the sale of our house. We had to make double payments, for our home in Airdrie as well as the one in Brooks. It also cost us to drive there every weekend and maintain the lawn and yard. We ended up selling it a few months later but for only $109,000.

As we started our new life in Airdrie we did not have anyone to take care of our kids. We were already stretched financially due to all the things that had happened with our house in Brooks. So we ended up taking our kids to work with us. Our parents were not around to help us at this point. I do not want to paint my parents with a dark brush and make them out to be bad people though. I loved my father very much and I absolutely forgave him for giving me up to foster care. I have also forgiven my mother, and we have become very close over the past few years. Brenda and I go and visit my mother and stepfather regularly and talk with them on the phone. They have come to our house and done things for us. One time my stepfather fixed the tiles in our bathroom. It took half a day to do that. Another time he helped me install my garage door opener. One time my mother came to our house and helped Brenda organize the food in the kitchen cupboards and pantry. I thank God for giving me grace to have such a great relationship with my mother now. If I had not forgiven her I would have missed out on knowing such wonderful people (Mom and her husband). I thank God for creating and enabling the process of forgiveness.

17 - The Accident

In August 2000 I was driving down the road in Bragg Creek doing my route. As I proceeded through an intersection a lady turned left in front of me, cutting me off. I tried to swerve to miss the vehicle but I hit it. I hit my head on the steering wheel as I impacted her car because my airbag did not deploy. My son Roman was riding with me that day. After I stopped I looked over at him and asked if he was okay, and he said that he was.

I got out and walked over to the other vehicle. I was shaking and was getting a headache. I asked the two ladies in the other vehicle if they were okay, and they told me that they were fine. I called the police, and they said if nobody was hurt and the vehicles were drivable to just drive to the repair shop and fill out an accident report later. So I called my boss to let him know what had happened, and he came out and finished my route. Then I crept my van, which was leaking all kinds of fluids everywhere, to the autobody shop. I called my wife and she came to my rescue. I was given a rental vehicle, and then my wife and I went to the hospital so that I could get looked at by a doctor.

We waited for about two hours and then were told that it would be about another two and a half hours or so, so we went home because we had to work the next day. I had excruciating pain in my head from the impact.

When I woke up the next morning it was even worse. My head hurt so bad that I took painkillers all day long. I also had trouble remembering places on my route that were very familiar to me. I had to keep calling my boss and asking him for directions. It was very frustrating.

The accident happened on a Thursday, and on Saturday I finally got X-rays done on my neck and head. The radiologist noted that I had broken the sixth bone in my neck in at least three places. I had begun to feel the effects of whiplash on my neck and back. I also had severe pain behind my eyes.

I had to go to get chiropractic and massage treatments every day for about ten months. I still kept running three miles a day and doing push-ups and stretches to try and ease the pain and discomfort in my neck and head.

It was very stressful for my family because I was in so much pain. I was miserable, because I had to work even though the pain was severe. I was a contractor and had not paid into Workers Compensation, so I was not entitled to receive benefits from them. If I had quit working, we would have lost our vans and house.

Our children started the new school year at the Christian school. I would drive them there and then my wife would pick them up after school. Our beautiful dalmation was also reunited with us once again. She was always so excited to be with us.

Many times in the middle of the night my wife would wake to me clawing at the curtains, and I would not know where I was. She would have to talk me back to bed or try to calm me down. It was scary for me to wake up and not know where I was sometimes. This had been going on since before we were married. My wife started to suggest that I should get counselling. I denied that I needed to go for counselling and claimed that everything was all right. But she persisted, and eventually, in November of 2000, we started to go for counselling.

It was about a forty-five-minute drive to the counsellor's office in Calgary. He was a Christian counsellor, and he dealt mostly with my anger issues and my thinking that every time I did something wrong God wanted to kill me or punish me. We attended these sessions for about a year. When the year was over I felt that some of the more profound issues that plagued me had been dealt with, even though I was still not convinced that God actually had a favourable disposition toward me. It would take four more years and a book by Joel Osteen to convince me that God was for me and not against me.

I was still having horrible thoughts that God wanted to kill me and to punish me for things I was doing wrong. I still lived in terrible fear that God was going to get me. I did not understand anything about God's loving character or how patient He is with His children. I still thought He was like Alice, my foster mother.

On the anniversary of my father's death I went to Medicine Hat to see my stepmother and family. We met at my stepmother's place and then went to the cemetery. We stayed there for a couple of hours and talked while looking at my father's tombstone.

In May of 2001 I took my van to a car dealership in Airdrie to get the oil changed. Then I picked up my vehicle and parked it in my driveway. The next morning I was driving down the road when the engine oil light came on. I pulled over and opened the hood. I pulled the dipstick out, and it was bone dry. I looked under the vehicle where the oil pan was and could not see the oil plug. It appeared to me that the person who did the oil change had not tightened the oil plug back in the pan, and all of the oil leaked out.

I called the dealership and let them know what had happened. They sent a tow truck to get my van, and then I had to go and get a rental van to do my route. They ended up having to rebuild the engine in my van as a result of their incompetence.

On June 28, 2001, I was doing my courier route and was almost back at the terminal. I was waiting at a set of lights when I heard the sound of tires skidding briefly behind me, and then the van was hit by a vehicle. I was pushed forward and felt the impact immediately.

Almost instantly I felt pain behind my eyes. Within an hour I had a very bad headache and felt nauseated. The police came to the accident scene, and I filled out a report for them. The car that hit me was wrecked. The whole front end was demolished. I later learned that the driver was going about 45 miles per hour when he struck my vehicle.

My recovery had progressed very slowly, and this would be a major setback for me. I went to the doctor after I left the accident scene, and he prescribed painkillers. The next morning when I woke up it was like I was reliving my first accident all over again. I experienced the same pain and symptoms as before, and now there were some new ones. I went back to work the next day because if I did not I would have lost my house and vehicle. But I had to get help with lifting boxes when doing my route. I also took painkillers all day for weeks on end.

In August of 2001 I took a day off on the long weekend,

and we went camping with our children for three days. We met up with my sister, Keri, her husband, Chuck, and their two kids, Billy and Ben. My sister and her husband have a great sense of humour and are fun to hang out with. We all had a great time. We played Frisbee in the lake as we swam, and we played soccer with the kids. At night we had campfires and talked while our kids watched the flames and put sticks in the fire. We also had absolutely beautiful weather for all three days. It was such a great way to get away from all of the stress we were under at home.

School started for our kids a week later. We had taken them out of the Christian school and put them in public school. My children were now in an all-year school, so they only had six weeks off in the summer. In spite of all the stress that my family was under, my children still were getting good grades in school. But life was becoming more and more stressful for my children, to the point of being almost unbearable. I was miserable because of the pain I was in and took out my frustration on my wife and children. I also still had many issues to deal with from the foster home. So in October of 2001 I started going to counselling in Airdrie to deal with life issues related to the physical abuse and how it had impacted me. The counsellor in Calgary had helped me considerably with the faith issues I had incurred from the foster home. But I needed a different counsellor to help me with the practical issues I was dealing with.

The counsellor was very skilled and detailed as he helped me work through the problems from the abuse. He helped me to see that Alice must have been mistreated very badly herself, which compelled her to treat me so poorly. Abuse perpetuates abuse, and anger perpetuates anger. Every Tuesday I would go to counselling for two hours. Reliving the abuse in order to deal with it made me extremely angry, and when I went home afterwards I was impossible to deal with.

I told the counsellor about many times when I was beaten horribly or witnessed others being beaten and how there was no adult to protect us or administer justice. Then I would bring my counselling session home with me. My poor wife and kids bore the brunt of my frustration as I replayed and dealt with the abuse to try and get over it. I faithfully went for counselling for two years.

Shortly after I started my counselling in October of 2001 we had a fire in our house. My wife and I were in the basement. She was doing laundry and I was doing paperwork. She had been watching a movie upstairs with our younger son, Roman and she was downstairs during a commercial. All of a sudden Roman yelled to us, very panicked, and told us to come upstairs. My wife had lit three candles in an ornamental centrepiece. It had plastic leaves for decoration, and they had caught on fire.

I bolted up the stairs as fast as I could and saw the whole centrepiece ablaze. I instinctively grabbed it, opened the front door, and threw it out into the snow. But as I did that, hot wax dripped on the floor and melted into the carpet in a path that led to the door. Thankfully that was all that happened. If Roman had not been upstairs, who knows if we would still have a house or not? God sure looked after us so that our home did not burn down. Our house insurance covered the carpet that had been damaged, but we ended up having to get all of the carpet in our home replaced so that it would match the new carpet in the living room.

When Christmas came my wife and I decided to stay at home with our kids to play games with them all day. We got up early to open presents with them. We always put a bunch of surprises into stockings for each other as well as presents under the tree. We let our children monopolize all of our time that day. We did not eat our turkey supper until 10 p.m. But our children remember that as one of the best Christmases ever.

On the weekends Brenda and I would always get up and have coffee together. We would spend time talking to each other for a couple of hours in the morning and plan our day. I never want to be so busy that I cannot spend time with my wife and children.

January 2002 rolled around, and I was still in terrible pain every day. If I slept in the wrong position my neck and head would start hurting and the pain would wake me up. When I got up in the morning I had a headache. When I came home from work at night it felt like my spine was on fire. I was still running three miles a day, doing push-ups, sit-ups and stretches to help me get better. I was also going to the gym twice a week to lift weights for my back problems.

One day in early January my mother phoned me and told me that my aunt had died in the clinic while getting checked over by the doctor. She had been battling cancer and was getting chemotherapy treatments. Her husband was my mom's brother.

About four weeks later I got another call. My grandmother—my mom's mom—had passed away. So in about four weeks my Uncle Gerald had lost his wife and his mother. I felt so sorry for him.

I always used to call my grandmother on the phone and talk to her. I would always make her laugh. I never heard her say anything unkind to anyone. Her husband had died before I was even born, so I cannot imagine how difficult it must have been going through life alone like that.

In April my condition worsened, and so on May 3, 2002, I was forced to quit my job due to the pain from my accidents. I did not know what I was going to do in order to make the payments on my house and vehicle. At least Brenda was still working. I would have to find another job that was not so physically demanding on my neck and head.

Shortly after I quit my job as a courier I became very fearful of driving or riding in a vehicle. Sometimes Brenda would be driving down the road, and as we were going through an intersection where we had the right of way, another vehicle would be coming up to the corner. I would panic and think that they would not stop and would hit us. I would yell to Brenda to hit the brakes. My condition became so insidious that I had to see a psychologist in Calgary for counselling for six months so that he could help me to drive again without being so paranoid.

In June I was praying quite a bit and really felt that I should fast and pray to try and get some answers from God. We just seemed to be having more and more problems hit us every day. Sometimes I was afraid to answer the phone because I thought someone was bringing us more bad news. So on June 30 I stopped eating. I did not eat again until August 2, 2002. I fasted for thirty-two days and did not eat any food at all during that time. I tried to spend as much time praying to God as I could. I had some visions from the Lord and also led two people to the Lord during my time of fasting.

I looked for another job for two months but could not find one that did not require lifting over fifty pounds. The bills started to pile up, and life became more stressful. I applied for a job at the City of Airdrie public works department, and I ended up getting hired on July 10, 2002.

Some days it was very difficult to fast. I was doing a physically laborious job. Sometimes I had to dig with a shovel or haul wood and signs around. I had diarrhea for about thirty days in a row. But God gave me the grace to go through all of the problems I encountered while fasting.

I thought I would get immediate results after I fasted, but my timetable does not always coincide with God's timetable. I wanted results to aid my ailing finances. My wage at the City of Airdrie was a quarter of what I had made as a contract courier. We had just finished paying off a $5,000 business loan in May. But we still had other bills for the business.

One early morning in August Brenda got a call from her courier boss. He said that she was being let go. Her route had doubled in size since she had started, and she had asked for more money to compensate for that and for the rising fuel costs. But the bosses did not want to pay her more, so they hired another contractor to do the route for the same wage that Brenda had been doing it for. But he could not keep up and do as many deliveries as Brenda had, so they had to hire a second courier to help him. They should have kept Brenda and paid her more money.

After Brenda lost her job, life became even more stressful due to our financial situation. Our children felt the crunch as well. Gradually we began to fall behind more and more on our payments. We were about three months behind on our gas payments, and the gas was shut off. Brenda borrowed money from her stepmother so that we could get it turned back on.

In September our beloved dog, Princess Dakota, died of stomach complications. She had swallowed a foxtail weed and choked on it. It caused her stomach lining to separate, and she died as a result of her coughing so much and so hard. She was the longest-standing running partner I had ever had.

Our finances were worse than ever. At Christmastime we did not have any money to buy presents for our kids or for each other. We had to go and get vouchers from Social Services and use them to buy gifts. I was very depressed, because I was supposed to be the provider and here we were broke at Christmas. My stepmother, Judy, sent us $300 as a gift. At that time it seemed like a million dollars to us. We used it to buy some presents for our kids. God had provided for us again.

We stayed home again that Christmas and played games all day with our kids. Despite our financial situation, at least we could be together at Christmas. I was thankful that things were not worse and that we were all healthy. It still ended up being a great Christmas.

In January my boss at the City of Airdrie informed me that there was no more money left in the budget to support my job, so I had to go work in the recycling department. My new job was very simple; too simple. People would bring their used cardboard to the recycling place and put it in a bin. I would take it out of the bin and put it in a hydraulic press to compact it. When the bale of cardboard was big enough, I would tie it off and start all over. It was absolutely mind-numbing work. Sometimes I would joke to the people at my job and say things like "I might not be working here very much longer." They would have a concerned look on their faces and ask why I was leaving. Then I would say, "Oh, didn't you hear what happened? I bought a lottery ticket." They would all start to laugh at my joke.

Sometimes I would say things like "I need to go to see my addiction counsellor because things are getting worse."

With concern they would ask what I was having trouble with, and I would say something like "Gummy bears and jujubes." It just made my job easier when I was in a state of good humour and making light of my situation instead of feeling sorry for myself. Feeling sorry would not do anything for me anyway.

Sometimes having a poor outlook on life causes physiological problems as well. I was watching a documentary where physicians figured that up to two-thirds of people's health problems originate from psychological problems.

On Saturdays I was in charge of running the transfer site where people brought all of their garbage. I would direct the people to the proper bins to put their trash in, take their money, and when the bins were full I would compact the garbage with a backhoe.

But we were still falling behind on our bills so I applied for a part-time job driving a truck on the weekends to make extra money. I would leave from Calgary on Saturday night at about 6:30 and drive to Regina. Then in the morning I would unload a forty-eight-foot trailer of food and drive to Saskatoon in the afternoon. With an empty trailer I would wait there until Monday morning and load pallets of flour to bring back to Calgary. My job at the city did not start until Tuesday, so it worked out quite well. The only problem was that I rarely saw my family.

Our finances were still causing us untold grief and making life very stressful for us. In February my sister and brother-in-law drove from Edmonton to our house with boxes of food. They did not call before they came; they just showed up at our door and blessed us. I was absolutely taken back and could not believe what they had done for us. Our money was stretched so tightly that we did not have very much to buy food with.

Brenda had also started some new jobs. She was working part-time at Macs as a cashier, part-time at the post office sorting mail, part-time doing janitorial work, and part-time selling makeup. Despite our having so many jobs and working so hard, we still continued to fall behind on our bills. We just were not making the money we had made at the courier business and had trouble paying the bills from our business.

I had talked to Brenda many times about perhaps retraining through DeVry to do something less physically demanding, like electronic engineering. She was all for it, so we talked with one of the counsellors about their program and about financing for it. We managed to get most of the funding through bursaries and grants so that I would not have to pay back so much at the end of my courses.

So on July 12, 2003, I started attending DeVry. I had quit the city of Airdrie job on June 7, 2003. I would go to classes at DeVry from 8 a.m. to 1 p.m., Monday to Friday, and then do homework for six to seven hours. On Friday nights I would go drive a truck. I worked forty hours on the weekends.

I was still going to see my counsellor on Tuesday nights for two hours. But stress at home was at an all-time high. There was so much yelling and anger that it seemed impossible to have any peace. Our finances were stretched to the limit, and there appeared to be no relief in sight. My wife and I were tithing and praying for relief, but it did not come. We had reached our breaking point.

On December 1, 2003, my wife and I declared bankruptcy. We went to a trustee in Calgary and filled out paperwork for our creditors. We gave up both of our vans, which we had paid

$40,000 into. Before my accidents we had gotten many loans for our business, mortgage, vehicles, and personal loans as well. We had always paid them off and had perfect credit. Now we lost our ability to obtain credit.

At Christmas we were completely broke. We had no money to buy anything at all. One of the people I had worked with at the city of Airdrie and two of his friends and their wives were looking for a family to help out, and we ended up being the recipients of their great generosity. They questioned us about what kinds of things we liked and then went out and bought presents individually for each person in our family. I had tremendous difficulty accepting help from these people, especially being the breadwinner in our home. But there was nothing I could do to improve my situation, so I humbly accepted their kind gesture. I ended up getting some wonderful presents too. God had miraculously provided for us again. He is an infinite God, and He can provide for anybody in an infinite number of ways.

Since that time my wife and I have become very close friends with all three couples. We get together regularly and play cards or volleyball. At Christmas we always get together and visit or have a gift exchange with $10 presents. They are wonderful people and so much fun to be with.

18 - Separated

January 2004 came, and the tension in our home grew worse and worse due to our financial situation and the constant pain I was in from the accidents. Brenda and I fought more and more frequently, and by the middle of March I could not take it any more. On March 17, 2004, I announced to Brenda and my kids that I was leaving.

I packed up some of my things, and a friend came to pick me up as I no longer had a vehicle. He let me stay with him for a few months. Brenda's father had given her a truck to drive, and we eventually paid him for it. She had been hired as a full-time contractor for the post office and needed the vehicle to do her mail route. She drove to many of the businesses in Airdrie and delivered their mail. She is such a hard-working woman.

I continued to go to DeVry on the weekdays and then work on the weekends. When I arrived back in town on Sunday night I had to walk three miles with my clothes and bedding to the bus stop. At least I was getting some exercise by walking that far. I was also still running three miles a day and doing push-ups and stretches to try to heal my head, neck, and back. I was also getting very high marks at DeVry despite all of the stress that I was dealing with.

On payday I would deposit half of my cheque into

Brenda's account so that she had money for the bills and food. Even though we were fighting, I was not malicious towards her. I did not want to make things even more difficult for her than they already were.

On Saturdays when I did not have to work until the afternoon I would go to my house in Airdrie to visit with Joel and Roman. Sometimes I would help the kids with schoolwork or projects like building things for their science classes. Other times Brenda and I would attempt to talk about problems we were having to try to sort out our conflicting issues with each other. On Mother's Day I took my kids out and we bought Brenda a bouquet of flowers, some chocolates, and a card. She thought that we had forgotten about Mother's Day, so she was very surprised when we presented the gifts to her.

In June I went to the Calgary Counselling Centre to get some help with my emotional problems. I recieved counselling for my anger and other problems with Brenda for about a month. Progress was very slow though. My counsellor introduced me to a program starting up called Responsible Choices. I enrolled in the course, which was about six months long, and attended all of the classes, once a week for two hours. I was the only person who came voluntarily. The other people had been ordered by a judge to attend due to abusing or assaulting their spouses. But we all seemed to have similar problems with our anger.

Brenda and I had also started going to marriage counselling once a week for three hours. We talked about our problems while the counsellor served as a mediator. Many problems had gone unresolved in our marriage, and it seemed as if we would never be able to resolve them. Some of this was because I had worked so many hours in the past that they did not get dealt with properly or at all. But in spite of all our problems, on July 1, 2004, I moved back home.

Even though I had all of this stress in my life I somehow managed to maintain a 3.0 average at DeVry and had a straight A average in all my electronic labs. I absolutely loved the lab classes and enjoyed building electronic devices.

In August Benny Hinn came to Calgary for a weekend crusade. I had heard about him and wanted to go to the crusade to see what it was about. The Friday morning at the crusade was set aside for just praise and worship. I wanted to try to get back on track with God, especially after all of the problems that I had been through with my family. I really wanted to touch God and at the same time have God touch my life. So I went to the service to just worship the Lord and sing praises to Him.

As I worshipped God and lifted my hands in the air tears rolled down my eyes. I am not a person who relies on feelings as I serve God. My feelings can deceive me into believing that God is not with me if I feel bad or upset. But I sensed the presence of the Lord in an overwhelming way that morning as I worshipped Him. It was like God was saying to me, "Greg, I know what you have been through, but I still love you very much and never did stop loving you through all of the bad times. I have not deserted you or abandoned you in your time of greatest hardship. I have been with you all along."

I really felt encouraged that morning as I spent time in the presence of the Lord. I knew that I needed to make more changes in my life spiritually and emotionally. I needed to deal with my children in a way that was more gentle and loving. God showed me a picture of a gentle, loving man who was patient, soft-spoken, and nurturing toward his family. "That person is you," God impressed upon me.

Tears welled up in my eyes as I thought about that picture. Then I became angry and said, "I could never be that person. It would be impossible for me to become that man."

There had been times when I told my wife that I wished she had said no when I asked her to marry me, not because I did not love her but because I thought she and my children would have been light years ahead if they had a different husband and father who was nurturing and better prepared than I to raise a family. My family would have had better financial opportunities with a man who was more prepared to start a family as well. I never realized how different I was until I observed how other fathers treated their kids. They were more nurturing, careful, and patient. I always felt so impetuous when dealing with my family.

I was still going to my Responsible Choices group every Thursday night. Sometimes I would leave the group frustrated because I did not feel I was getting any solid counsel or advice on how to do things differently. Some weeks the men would all talk about their week and how they responded to particular circumstances that frustrated them. I would also talk about my week, but I felt like my anger was always about four or five notches higher on the scale than theirs.

As I look back on my life after I came out of the foster home, I realize that over the years God has slowly whittled away my anger from seething rage that lasted for weeks at a time to where it is at now. I am not that person any more. My anger does not control me like it used to. But it took twenty-five years (a quarter of a century) to get to this point.

It is frustrating for me that it took so long to get better. I do not believe that I have arrived at a place where I can quit seeking to become even better than I am now.

While at the Benny Hinn crusade we had heard an announcement regarding the Jubilee Christian Centre. We were looking for a new church, and we decided to visit that church and try it out. So the next Sunday we went to the Jubilee Christian Centre. The people seemed very friendly and warm. My wife and I especially liked the praise and worship because it was what we were used to. After the service we were invited to a hotel to meet other people from the church. We spent a few hours there and really felt welcomed.

My wife and I also started going to a cell group, a weekly gathering of a small group for Bible study and prayer. It was encouraging to get together with people to visit and share our time.

In my fourth semester at DeVry I quit truck driving and started working at a warehouse moving freight. The freight was on the floor, and my job was to stack it onto pallets so that it could be stored properly. It was also mind-numbing work, but at least I was working. I still did not have a vehicle, so I walked from DeVry to the warehouse, about two miles away. I am thankful it was so close to where I was going to school.

It was now the beginning of October 2004. I talked with Brenda about our finances and decided that at the end of October I would not return to DeVry. I felt like I needed to focus on my finances and try to rebuild them so that we were not struggling so hard. I felt like it would also take some stress off of our marriage.

My family is very important to me. Each time one of my sons had a birthday I would take them out for lunch and visit with them one on one. I wanted my sons to know that they were very important to me. I always wanted to take special time for them. My sons are both grown now and I am so proud of them. They are such a joy to be around and so creative and funny. I love hanging around with them as we joke with each other.

At the end of October I started a job at a business in Airdrie, making $8 an hour. It was the only work I could find at that time, especially since I did not have a vehicle. I worked there for almost two months doing light deliveries and other duties. I also applied for a paper route and started delivering newspapers every morning from 4 to 6 a.m. I wanted to make sure that I had extra money to purchase Christmas presents for my family. I used to tell people that I was the CEO of Greg's Paper Delivery, just to add some humour to my situation. It always got a good laugh.

In December I applied for a truck driving job in Calgary. I got the job and worked from 1 p.m. until 10 p.m. doing pickups and deliveries in Calgary. It was not great money, but it at least helped with the bills. The problem with this job was that I had to lift boxes all day long, which took a toll on my neck and head.

After Christmas I applied for a truck driving job doing long hauls again across Canada and the USA. I went to work at the end of January, and I was usually gone for twenty-six days a month. I would drive an average of 500 miles per day. It was very difficult for Brenda to try to manage everything on her own. It was also difficult to try to rebuild our relationship when I was 3,000 miles away. Our marriage relationship was quite tenuous, and we were still not sure that it would survive at this point. At least I was making better money than at my last job.

Whenever I made it back home on my days off I tried to

get to church and Bible study. I really missed being around other Christians and still had a real hunger for the Lord and the Word of God. During that year doing long hauls I began a mission to learn more of the Word of God and devoted myself to memorizing the Bible. I already knew a great deal of Scripture but knew that to be more effective as a Christian and win many of the battles in my mind I would need to know more of the Word of God. I ended up memorizing all of Galatians, Ephesians, Philippians, Colossians, 1 Thessalonians, 2 Thessalonians, 1 Timothy, 2 Timothy, Titus, Philemon, Hebrews, James, 2 Peter and 2 John. I memorized all of the verses of fourteen books of the Bible. I still have a hunger to know more of the Word of God.

During my days off I also tried very hard to spend as much time with my wife and kids as I could. Sometimes on a Sunday afternoon we would all get together and play board games or get ice cream and visit. Other times we would rent movies and watch them together.

My wife was having trouble with our children though. They were not listening to her as well as they should have been. She needed me closer to home so that I could help her with the kids. So on October 21, 2005, I quit my job driving a truck. Before getting into my accidents I had only had two jobs in seven years. Now I had gone through six jobs in the past two and a half years. It was difficult starting over every four to six months while trying to find a job that did not take me away from home so much or that did not cause me to have terrible headaches.

In November I started doing home renovations with a friend I had been playing volleyball with. We completely stripped an apartment and then rebuilt it. We had to move the cupboards and then retile the kitchen. We also put new drywall into the bathroom. I was not an expert at renovating, so I asked lots of questions to make sure the job I did looked professional.

In December I started two new jobs. One job was backing 48' trailers into bays at a warehouse from 6:30 to 2:30 p.m. Then from 3:30 p.m. until midnight I worked at ATCO doing electrical wiring. I only did the two jobs for a couple of weeks so that I could make enough money to buy presents for Christmas again. Then I quit the truck-driving job.

I was really enjoying working at a job that did not involve driving. The people I met at my new job were just great to work with too. At coffee time I loved to sit and joke with them about life. Humour was still my favourite drug to help me get through rough times. When life was crumbling in front of my eyes I could always find something humorous to joke about. The more ridiculous it was, the better I liked it. I love to be sarcastic in a gentle way and banter with other people. It is very cathartic for me. If I was doing a job that I did not like, I would make it fun by joking so it was easier to get through the day. That has become a great coping mechanism in my life. I have tried to pass this onto my children and it has worked for them too.

When I was growing up there were times when I would be drinking a beverage and accidentally spill it. My parents would get angry and make a big deal out of it, probably because it was an inconvenience to clean up the mess. But when my kids were growing up I would purposely bump their arms and make them spill their drinks. Then I would say something like "Way to go, clumsy." Then I would proceed to help them clean it up. I wanted them to know that spilling a drink was not a big deal. I did many things like this with my children and always tried to incorporate as much humour in my relationship with them as I could.

Both of my children are intelligent and have a great sense of humour. Whenever possible my wife and I would teach our children. Sometimes I would be watching a movie with my family and I would pause the movie to teach my kids something about physics, chemistry, biology, etc. As a result our children are very knowledgeable about many things compared to us at their age.

I worked at ATCO for almost a year. I was learning a great deal about how to run electrical wires to power devices in a house. I was also learning what kinds of wire to use and how to read blueprints. It was great to be home every night with my family, but we were still struggling financially due to my low-paying job. I would get paid one day, and the next day after my tithe, mortgage, groceries, and power bills were paid there was hardly any money left in my account. It was extremely frustrating for me to still be having so much difficulty with our finances.

Again I started looking for another job. I put my letters of recommendation together with my resume and faxed a bunch of trucking companies who were looking for drivers. I received a call one day from a company in Grande Prairie. I talked to the manager on the phone for a while and was told the starting wage. It was ten dollars more per hour than what I was making. There would also be a raise after sixty days if I passed my probation period. I already had five years experience at this kind of work.

I jumped at the chance and within a week was on my way to Grande Prairie to start my new job. I had planned to come home once a month for a week so that I would not spend as much money on gas to go back and forth. The first time I went up I worked thirty-five days straight and then came home for my days off. My first paycheque was two and a half times my paycheque at ATCO. The company also had great medical and dental benefits. I have been with the same company for three years. I had started out in 2004 with a job making $8 an hour. Now I was making much more than that. It pays to be persistent.

"Never give up," is my motto in life. We need to persevere and not give up. Sometimes we think that we have fought as hard as we can for as long as we can to overcome some crisis or problem and we end up giving up. The truth is, we have fought long and hard for seven rounds. But we still have five more rounds to go until the fight is over, and then we will be victorious. Do not give up halfway through the fight.

Sometimes when I was struggling to control my thought life, especially when thoughts of unforgiveness would assail me, I would say, "Jesus, I give you these bad thoughts." Sometimes I would say that prayer many times in a row to try and control my thought life. Did I eventually gain control of my thought life? The answer is yes, because I fought so hard for so long. It took months of doing that to eventually be victorious.

If I had given up, I would never have gotten my job in Grande Prairie. If I had given up, I would never have had the opportunity to rebuild my relationship with my mother and father. I would never have gotten back together with my darling bride, Brenda. We have a fantastic relationship now. If I had given up and not gone to counselling I would never have known the emotional freedom that I now experience. If I could reiterate one phrase in this world it would be, "Never give up."

I have also continued to memorize the Word of God. The more I learn the Word of God, the more stability I have in my life. The Bible helps me to understand more of what God thinks and how He responds in many situations of my life and in my walk with Him.

I have spent a great deal of time trying to rebuild my relationship with my wife and children. I believe that we all have a better relationship now than we have ever had before. But I have had to put a tremendous amount of effort into obtaining knowledge of how to do this. I have spent three exhausting years in counselling, taken two anger management programs, and read countless books on how to improve my communication and relationships with other. I know that I still have a long way to go, but I believe the worst is over. I know that without having Jesus in my life I would have not been able to get through all of the things that weighed my family and me down. God was there all along to help us through the toughest times of our lives.

19 - New and Improved

My family and I have turned a corner since I started working at my latest job. Life has become more bearable in many ways as time has gone on. My family has had to overcome many things as we endured years of hard times. But I feel that it has made us better Christians and stronger people. I have compassion for people who go through tough circumstances. I am a more understanding person and it has changed who I am.

I try to be a man of principle, so there are a number of things I do. First of all, I always look for the beauty in people. A person might be overweight but have long, dark, gorgeous eyelashes or a very beautiful smile. Another person might appear to be unkempt in their appearance but have a very warm, caring, loving way about them. If we look for the bad we will find it. If we look for the good we will find it. I try to enjoy my life everyday. Sometimes people say to themselves, *When I get a car I will be able to enjoy my life.* Don't wait for some event to occur before you think you can enjoy life. It might never come.

When someone takes time to create a beautiful work of art, others come from around the world to admire it. If a person criticized or insulted that artwork, the person who created it would be very hurt. I do not want to criticize or insult God's greatest work of art, human beings, who are made in His image. I do not want to hurt God's feelings, because He took so much pride in His work. When we are inconvenienced or hurt by other people's actions we need to be quick to forgive and not insult or hurt those people. God is watching our every response. Proverbs 19:11 says, "*A man's wisdom gives him patience; it is to his glory to overlook an offense.*" I try to not be petty and unforgiving. I want to be bigger than that.

I always treat people with dignity and respect regardless of their profession. If I am in the grocery store, I do my best to treat the checkout person with respect. If there is a long lineup I will say to that person, "How are you today, hard working lady?" instead of chewing her out for taking so long with the other orders and people. It is not her fault that there is a labour shortage. I usually get a smile from her, and hopefully it makes her day. I want to be a man who drips with grace for other people. That act of love will show them more of who God is than my bad temper will.

Secondly, I always compare myself to people who have less than me instead of those who have more than me, because it makes me appreciative instead of ungrateful.

Thirdly, I try to understand who God really is and have a proper perspective of Him. God does not hate worldly people because they are worldly; He loves them very much. He gave His life for those people, and so I need to love them as much as I possibly can as well. I do this not by my words but by my actions. They need to see the Bible in action, not just hear about it. Romans 13:8 says, "…he who loves his fellowman has fulfilled the law."

God is not who we think He is. He is so much more. He is so much more full of grace and love than we are. His love endures forever, and nothing can separate us from that love, just as it says in Romans 8:35-39. When I mess up, God is saying, "Get up and try again. I love you and want you to keep moving forward. I know that you are not perfect, but I still love you and want you to do the best that you can." He is not saying, "Oh man, this is the last time I'm going to forgive you! You have messed up way too much, and I cannot take it any more. Next time is the last time, and then I am going to let you have it." God never says that to His children. People say this to each other, but our Gracious Father does not. He is much more patient, enduring, and loving than people are.

Fourthly, when my wife needs my help I never say no. I always try to help her with the housework and do the dishes or mop the floor. I help my kids with their homework and school projects. I want to be as much a part of my home and family as I possibly can. This is part of what living is all about. I am the head of the house as a leader, not a dictator. A leader does what is best for his followers. A dictator does what is best for himself. My wife is not my slave; she is my partner whom I love and cherish.

Lastly, if there is something that is troubling me, I pray about it. ":Is any one of you in trouble? He should pray..." (James 5:13). Christ came to set us free so that we can live in freedom (John 8:36). I believe that I am freer now than I have ever been. I have forgiven all of the people who have hurt me in my past. I pray for my foster mother, foster father, and Miles. I have a great relationship with my mother and stepfather. I do not believe that I have one enemy in this world.

There are many things that we must do as we mature as Christians. But even if you are not a Christian and you are reading this you can still follow some of these principles because these are also things that we should be doing as we mature as adults. When we were very young our thinking was so egocentric. But as we matured our focus became more peripheral, directed toward other people and we hopefully learned to give and help others with our time, finances, etc. When people mature physically but not mentally they are sometimes labelled or viewed as dysfunctional.

Some people accept Christ into their lives and do not want to mature as Christians. Sometimes their ability to mature is stagnated by their behaviour or thought pattens. Many Christians do not feel like they have freedom in their lives and wonder why their prayers are not answered. There are many reasons for this.

First of all, a mature Christian is quick to forgive others when wronged or hurt. People get upset about this and argue that if they forgive that person that they will not pay for the wrong that they did. But that is actually a fallacy because those people will reap what they have sowed. God has set that spiritual law in place just like He has set physical laws in place. We do not doubt physical laws like gravity so why should we doubt spiritual laws? Pray for your enemies and it releases God to do what He has to do. Ultimately, our goal should not be to wish malice on people who have hurt us. We should want the best for them. It goes against our thinking so strongly but that is what God wants us to do. 1 John 4:20 says, *"If anyone says, 'I love God,' yet hates his brother, he is a liar. For anyone who does not love his brother, whom he has seen, cannot love God, whom he has not seen."*

Second, a mature Christian does not criticize or judge other people, ever! When we start comparing ourselves to others we become conceited or fault finding. God does not want us to be like that. Galatians 6:3-5 says, *"If anyone thinks he is something when he is nothing, he deceives himself. Each one should test his own actions. Then he can take pride in himself, without comparing himself to somebody else, for each one should carry his own load."*

Then in James 4:11 it says, *"Brothers, do not slander one another. Anyone who speaks against his brother or judges him speaks against the law and judges it. When you judge the law, you are not keeping it, but sitting in judgment on it."* So if I judge someone else for their sin, I am also sinning by judging them.

Third, it should always be our desire to pray for others when we have personality conflicts instead of criticizing them or arguing with them because we are not supposed to wrestle against flesh and blood. We are actually in a spiritual battle against the forces of the darkness. We need to fight the proper kind of fight or else we will never win. Ephesians 6:12 says, "*For our struggle is not against flesh and blood, but against the rulers, against the authorities, against the powers of this dark world and against the spiritual forces of evil in the heavenly realms.*"

Fourth, as mature Christians we need to always be in an attitude of thankfulness. We do not know what God has planned for us at all times. So when we go through hardships we need to understand that God is building our character so that we become people of greater character who can identify with other people in crisis and help them or pray for them. 1Thessalonians 5:18 says, "*give thanks in all circumstances, for this is God's will for you in Christ Jesus.*"

Finally, I need to understand God's character and opinion of me. God is full of love and only wants the best for me. When bad things happened in my life it was not because God caused them. He allowed the devil to have access to me, just like He did with Job in the Bible. Sometimes things happened to me because of my poor decisions. But God only wants the best for me like it says in James 1:17. "*Every good and perfect gift is from above, coming down from the Father of the heavenly lights, who does not change like shifting shadows.*" The devil, not God, comes to wreck my life. I also know that when I sin God looks to me and says, "I do not condemn you." I know this because that is how Jesus responded to the woman that the Pharisees caught in the act of adultery. When Jesus said, "*…neither do I condemn you*" (John 8:11), it was evident that He was forgiving her. It says in the Bible that "*Jesus Christ is the same yesterday and today and forever*" (Hebrews 13:8). If I am judged for my sin now, then I can never have forgiveness from Jesus because my sin will only be judged once. So He can never take my sin on Himself if He has already judged it.

The Bible says in Romans 12:2, "*Do not conform any longer to the pattern of this world, but be transformed by the renewing of your mind. Then you will be able to test and approve what God's will is—his good, pleasing and perfect will.*" So we need to change our thinking patterns to be more like God wants us to be. We cannot have the same thinking patterns as we used to because we are a new creation.

Does this give me a license to sin? Absolutely not! Hebrews 10:26-27 says, "*If we deliberately keep on sinning after we have received the knowledge of the truth, no sacrifice for sins is left, but only a fearful expectation of judgment and of raging fire that will consume the enemies of God.*" These verses are tied to 1 John 4:18, which says, "*There is no fear in love. But perfect love drives out fear, because fear has to do with punishment. The one who fears is not made perfect in love.*" Jesus said, "*If you love me, you will obey what I command*" (John 14:15). It is so interesting that Scripture gives us the answers we need if we just read it. If we are full of fear, perhaps we need to stop sinning and start loving others more.

I obey God and His commands because I love Him and do not want to hurt Him by my disobedience. I am compelled by my love relationship to do all that I can to show that I am in love with God. It is just the same as not wanting to hurt my wife or offend her. So I do all that I can to promote our loving relationship and not do things to hurt her. That is how I feel about God my Father. I love Him and have a great relationship with Him. I do not want to destroy the intimacy I have with Him. If I obey God out of fear that something bad will happen to me, then I am living by the law and do not have a relationship with God.

When we start to be transformed and not live like the world does, we can hear the voice of God so much clearer. We will also understand His will for our lives. It might not happen overnight. If it took years for us to get into some of our messes, it will probably take some time to change some of our habits. But God is very gracious and patient with us. He will give us wisdom and ability to change as we desire and strive to change. He is an infinite God with infinite ways to help us. The God who made more stars in the sky than all the grains of sand on all the beaches in all the world can surely help us with our problems. Just ask for His help today, and He will be faithful to help everyone who asks.

Having faith in God to answer our prayers is very much a waiting game. If I pray for something and see the results immediately I will conclude that God indeed answers my prayers. But suppose I am only willing to pray for four months, and God declares to Himself that He will answer that prayer in exactly six months. If I give up and declare that God does not answer prayer, I then erode my own faith because I do not persevere to the end. God's timing does not always coincide with mine. So I have to trust that God is working out my life according to what He thinks is best for me, not what I think is best for me. That is part of faith.

One time I was at a restaurant with my wife. A blind man and his wife were at another table. My wife knew the couple because she delivers the mail to them. I approached the table and asked the blind gentleman if I could pray for him. He agreed to let me pray for God to restore his vision. I did not put a deadline on God to heal him. Months went by, and one day my wife found out that the University of Calgary was doing an experiment and this man was chosen to get a stem cell implant to restore his vision. We do not know yet if it will work or not. I believe it will, because God answers my prayers. He is an infinite God with infinite resources to meet our needs.

God has used all of the bad things that happened to me in my past to make me stronger and more grateful. He has used the weaknesses that tormented me to make me a better person. I now have more compassion for hurting and broken people than ever before. I do not just know about their problems; I have experienced many of them. Instead of being bitter about my past circumstances and living my life complaining to God about how hard everything has been, I live with great appreciation for how much God has done for me and how He has delivered me from all of those problems that tormented me. "*If the Son sets you free, you will be free indeed*" (John 8:36). When I am obedient to God and have no hatred in my life, I live with freedom in my mind. That is what Christ came to accomplish in my life through His example and power.

Many people deceive themselves or are deceived and live their lives in total bondage. Ask yourself if you really are free or even feel free. Do thoughts of revenge or hate plague you? Do you have unforgiveness toward another person? Insanity is defined as "doing the same thing over and over while expecting different results."[1] Is that what you are doing? Ask God to give you wisdom to do things that will produce results.

You do not want to stay in a position of unforgiveness forever. If you are waiting for the other person to come to you, it might never happen. Why not make the first move and forgive him? A person forgives first with his will, and then his emotions follow that act. It is not the other way around. You cannot forgive when you feel like it, because those feelings might never come to you. Set yourself free and see what God has for you.

I do not want to waste my life thinking about my past. God has great things in store for me, and I want to be ready for what He has. I want to move into the promised land and live out what God is going to do through me. How can I possibly do this if I am bitter and not seeking the Lord with a clear heart and mind?

Someday I will die and go to heaven. I am sure that throughout the course of eternity I will sit down at a table and have coffee or tea with Jesus. He will ask me very personal questions about why I did or did not do certain things on earth when I had the chance. I do not want that to be a difficult time for me. I want Jesus to be overwhelmed with joy due to the fact that I did as much as I could to help others and be obedient to Him.

---

[1] *Cynical Quotations,* Michael Moncur -Quotation # 26032

Sometimes I ponder the power, character, and beauty of our awesome Creator. He is full of love, beauty, and generosity. He made everything perfect, with wonder and variety. He created many unique animals and gave them the ability to care for themselves. He made many wonderful foods for us to eat and enjoy. If we just stop and take time to look at creation, we will see the beauty and creativity that God possesses. It was all done for our enjoyment and pleasure. God is demonstrating to us His ability and power as an infinite God.

It has taken us lifetimes to explore the human body, outer space, flowers, trees, etc., that God created in six days. I believe that God can hold the entire universe in both hands and rotate it or move it however He wants. The Bible says that He set the stars in place (Psalm 8:3). How can we resist loving and wanting to get to know this beautiful being who is so powerful yet so full of love for us. Just look for yourself at His marvellous creation and you will see how God has provided everything we need and more for us.

www.ingramcontent.com/pod-product-compliance
Ingram Content Group UK Ltd.
Pitfield, Milton Keynes, MK11 3LW, UK
UKHW020655231225
9727UKWH00015B/88

9 781460 000274